"THE STORY OF JUBILEE"

AN EPIC TALE BASED ON TRUE EVENTS

BY JAMIMA BEATRICE JONES

To my husband, Paul who encouraged me to convert my original stage production into a novel, my three wonderful children; Mimi, Jemille and Jean-Paul, my biggest fans who convinced me that "The Story of Jubilee" has a place in the Arts world, and Selena James who was intrigued enough by my query to encourage me to see this manuscript through.

"THE STORY OF JUBILEE"

AN EPIC TALE BASED ON TRUE EVENTS

BY

JAMIMA BEATRICE JONES

APPROXIMATELY 112,447 WORDS

FOREWARD

After the freedom bell rang, the American Missionary Association and the Freedmen's Bureau joined forces and established the first public schools for the education of newly-freed slave children. The Fisk Free-Colored school was one of those institutions.

"The Story of Jubilee" is the epic tale of the key students that made up the original Fisk Jubilee Singers; namely Ella Sheppard, Maggie Porter, Frederick Loudin, Thomas Rutling and their Professor, George White.

George White, a White man from Cadiz, New York was never a singer, but was talented in interpreting music. An accomplished director, White directed choirs at schools and churches in Ohio, where he also founded a Black Sunday school. Having been medically discharged from the Freedmen's Bureau in Nashville, White showed up at the Fisk Free-Colored school to offer his assistance as a music teacher. He ultimately formed a group of singers on the campus in his spare time who he Christened the "Fisk Jubilee Singers".

Though the author is unknown, the chorus of "Swing Low, Sweet Chariot" was first ever sang at the near-drowning of Ella Sheppard at the hands of her own mother. Ella Sheppard is attributed with teaching the original Fisk Jubilee Singers this most revered song, and it is the first song ever recorded by African-Americans, as it was recorded by the four men of the original Fisk Jubilee Singers. When she became Professor White's Assistant, Ella became Fisk's first African-American teacher. Sheppard was an accomplished soprano, a pianist, and the original Assistant Director of the original Fisk Jubilee Singers.

Frederick Loudin was born free in Ravenna, Ohio. Though his family had been long-term members of a fine Methodist church, when a position to sing in the choir became available, Loudin attempted to audition for the position as an accomplished baritone only to be told that "Coloreds" were not allowed to sing in the church choir; freed slaves, non-slaves, it didn't matter. Loudin made acquaintance with Professor George White, and White invited him to join the original Fisk Jubilee Singers. He sang with the group during it's entire existence, even though he was older than the other students and had never enrolled as a student at the university. Loudin spent his entire career with the group vying for Ella Sheppard's position as the Professor's Assistant which caused great dissension between he, Ella Sheppard and Maggie Porter.

Thomas Rutling was almost separated from his family during a slave sale at the age of 3. Because his mother pleaded so earnestly for his life, the new master's daughter was successful in convincing her father to allow her to tend to the child while his mother worked the fields. As a result, Rutling and two of his siblings were reared and educated by this Mistress. Because he was educated, Rutling was a Surgeon's Assistant at the tender age of 11, and one of the first students to enroll in the newly-formed Fisk Free-Colored School at the age of 14. He arrived carrying a letter of reference from the Surgeon he assisted, who was friends with General Clinton B. Fisk.

As a child, Maggie Porter was often found on the church steps, listening to the choir sing. After enrolling into, and graduating from the Fisk Free-Colored School, Porter became the first African-American school teacher to graduate from the university. She taught at several schools that were burned down by the KKK. Though she regretted it over the years, Porter by-passed her own career as an opera singer when Professor White asked her to return to Fisk to become one of the original Fisk Jubilee Singers. At one point in time, Porter was banned from the group for 6 months because she couldn't get along with any of the other singers. She was the last surviving member of the original Fisk Jubilee Singers.

These students, along with their Professor, embarked on a journey to save the Fisk Free-Colored School from bankruptcy. Though the university scoffed at the idea when it was presented to them by the Professor, White raised $36 and took the students on tour, anyway. The school ultimately donated $1 to the cause.

The students originally followed the route of the Underground Railroad, but made little funds, though they were successful at the Masonic Hall (Home to Church of God In Christ) in Tennessee where they earned $400. They sang for President Ulysses S. Grant's inauguration, they were invited to England by Queen Victoria twice, and they toured the world several times earning a reputed $172,000 between 1871 and 1877. During these times, they became ill, the Professor's wife died and the university refused to allow them to return to the states because their efforts were keeping the university afloat. Those funds would be equivalent to roughly $3 million today, and not only saved the university, but were used to construct the first permanent structure for the education of African-Americans; Jubilee Hall on Fisk's campus. In that hall is a floor-to-ceiling mural of the original Fisk Jubilee Singers commissioned by Queen Victoria.

All Aboard.....

Jamima B. Jones,
Author/Playwright

"Whatever empowering story we haven't heard in the Black community, it's time to hear it."

Janelle Monae

CHAPTER ONE

On the morning of October 6,1871, an optimistic Professor George White and Pastor Henry

Bennett from the "Fisk Free-Colored School" waited at the train depot. Their wives dutifully

stood at their sides. Men, women and children of all ages had gathered on the streets, in the trees

and even on rooftops as early as dawn to get a glimpse of this most talked-about singing group of

Colored youngsters from Nashville's Fisk Free-Colored School. Word had spread that these

kids were historically being allowed to board the train and go on something called a "tour" to sing what folks referred to as "classical" music. Their friends and families didn't know what it all meant, but they knew it was something to be proud of, so they turned out in droves.

Several weeks before, Professor White had called a meeting with the children's parents who were reluctant to let their children leave town with the Professor.

"Where will our children stay? It ain't like they welcome at White folks' fancy hotels," one parent had stated.

"I have several friends and acquaintances in the Ohio area, and my wife, who will be traveling with us, has already made accommodations for the children's lodging. I assure you that your children will be safe and secure," White had avowed.

"And what about food? Our kids ain't used to the fancy food you White folks eat. How will you feed them?" someone else asked.

George White stood, adjusted his jacket and carefully chose his words. "I think it would be best if you pack rations of the foods your children prefer eating. I will have my wife make sure that everyone's rations are clearly labeled and kept fresh on blocks of ice."

The parents still shifted uneasily in their seats and whispered to one another. Pastor Henry Bennett sensed their uneasiness, slowly arose from his seat with distinction and walked toward the front of the room.

"Professor White, may I have a word with the parents?"

"Why, of course, Pastor Bennett. Please do."

Pastor Bennett rubbed his chin in contemplation before speaking. "Good evening. Most of you know me, but for those who do not, I am Pastor Henry Bennett." He paced up and down the rows of seats as he presented his position.

"I know you are all concerned about your children, and rightfully so. However, this is a wonderful opportunity for your children to see some of the country, and at the same time, save their beloved Fisk."

Most parents nodded their heads in agreement. A few folded their arms in protest, still unconvinced. Pastor Bennett continued.

"Professor White seems to have considered the critical requirements necessary to take the children on tour, in guaranteeing their lodging and how they will be fed. Now, if it would ease your minds even further, I would be willing to travel along with the group as a chaperone."

More of the doubters started to show signs of being converted, and all began to whisper among themselves. Sensing victory, Pastor Bennett went for the close.

"I will even take my wife along as a chaperone for your daughters. Now, with that said, do we have all of your consents?"

Every parent in the room nodded their heads, then put their marks on the paperwork before them as their doubtful faces changed to those of approval. Each parent was given the itinerary the students planned to follow, and the meeting was adjourned.

#

Founded on September 3, 1846 in Albany, New York, the "American Missionary Association" was a Protestant-based abolitionist group whose main purpose was to abolish slavery, educate newly-freed Coloreds, promote racial equality, and promote Christian values. Formerly known as the "Bureau of Refugees, Freedmen and Abandoned Lands", the "Freedmen's Bureau" was an agency of the United States Department of War formed on March 3, 1865, and was initiated by President Abraham Lincoln. It's goal was to oversee issues such as provisions, clothing, and fuel for the immediate and temporary shelter and supply of destitute and suffering refugees, freedmen

and their wives and children. After the Civil war ended, the Freedman's Bureau and the

American Missionary Association joined forces, and one of their most recognized

accomplishments was in education.

General Clinton B. Fisk was an abolitionist who was appointed Colonel of the 33rd

Missouri Volunteer Infantry of the Union Army on September 5, 1862. General Fisk was later

appointed Assistant Commissioner of the Freedmen's Bureau for Kentucky and Tennessee, and

he helped establish the first three public schools in the south for White and African-American

children. One of those schools was named for him; the Fisk Free-Colored School, to which he

endowed $30,000 and opened on January 9, 1866. In all, the Bureau spent $5 million to set up

these most historical schools, many of which are included on the list of Historical Black Colleges

(HBCs).

George White was born in Cadiz, New York in 1838. He was the son of a blacksmith

who played in a local band, and George had spent many hours watching and listening to his

father perform. In 1858 White moved to Ohio, and although not a singer himself, he developed

a talent for interpreting music. He began directing choirs at schools and churches, where he also

founded a Black Sunday school. He, thereafter, dedicated his career both to music and to

proving African-Americans were the social and intellectual equals of Whites. After serving in

the Union army at Gettysburg, Chancellorsville and Chattanooga, White's health was nearly

destroyed. Therefore, he was medically discharged and joined the Freedmen's Bureau in

Nashville.

Born of Quaker parents in Brownsville, Pennsylvania in 1838, Rev. Henry Stanley Bennett was graduated from Oberlin College in 1860 and from Oberlin Theological Seminary in 1863. He served as Pastor of the Congregational Church in Wakeman, Ohio from 1863 to 1867. Thereafter, he Pastored the church associated with the Fisk Free-Colored School, as well as served as a German and Theology Teacher at the university. Pastor Bennett was known to have a special intellect to guide the youth of emancipated people, and among Colored people, he was looked upon as a leader who could be implicitly trusted for advice that was for their best interests.

#

That crisp October morning in Nashville in 1871, the students had slowly arrived with their proud parents, siblings and friends and were taken aback by all of the fanfare as they walked the gauntlet toward the Professor, Pastor Bennett and their wives. The young men of the ensemble wore their best loafers, suits made from slave cloth, freshly-laundered cotton shirts, and borrowed bow ties. Their luggage, mere burlap bags, contained everything needed to endure the journey. The young women of the troupe arrived wearing ankle-length, cotton skirts with freshly-laundered, ruffled blouses.

Their families had prepared care packages for them of fried chicken, corn cobs and corn cakes. Some had even included candies, sweet tarts and desserts neatly stored in tin cans and burlap bags.

"Come along, come along everyone," the Professor instructed. "Let's get aboard and start on our journey to sing the money out of the hearts and pockets of the people."

Word had also gotten around that the students were touring because their school was in financial straits and they hoped their efforts would give the university a chance to succeed.

"All aboard," the conductor called out.

Everyone began to give their last hugs and kisses, and the students gathered around as Ella Sheppard suddenly began a round of :

"Get on board children,

Get on board children,

Get on board children,

There's room for plenty more."

A surprised Professor White turned, encouraged the students to form a straight line and began to direct them as they sang another round :

"Get on board children,

Get on board children,

Get on board children,

There's room for plenty more."

Just then, Maggie Porter came up with an idea, interlocked arms with Ella Sheppard and began to sway from side to side. The other students followed suit as Maggie blended in with:

"For there is plenty good room,

plenty good room,

plenty good room in my Father's kingdom.

Plenty good room,

plenty good room, so choose your seat and sit down."

Professor White smiled at the group, then encouraged Maggie to step forward and sing the solo:

"I would not be a sinner,

I tell you the reason why,

Because the Lord might call me,

And I wouldn't be ready to die. For there is…"

Maggie rejoined the others in line, then the group joined back in:

"Plenty good room, plenty good room,

plenty good room in my father's kingdom,

plenty good room, plenty good room,

so choose your seat and sit down."

Thomas Rutling suddenly broke away from the group and started a Charleston Shuffle which prompted the other students to do the same. Rutling chimed in with:

"I'm gonna lay down my sword and shield,"

The other students answered him:

"Down by the riverside, down by the riverside, down by the riverside."

Thomas called to them again:

"I'm gonna lay down my sword and shield."

They answered back:

"Down by the riverside, and study war no more."

Professor White beamed with pride as he directed Ella Sheppard to start up the stairs of the train. The group followed as Ella brought the medley full-circle:

"So get on board children,

Get on board children,

Get on board children,

There's room for plenty more."

The other singers climbed the stairs of the huge locomotive and gathered alongside Ella on the caboose, in front of the rail. They waved to their loved-ones who jeered and cheered and waved their hankies. Professor White directed the students to end the song, and they did:

"Get on board children,

Get on board children,

Get on board children,

There's room for plenty more."

All except Maggie Porter. Not to be upstaged, Maggie stepped forward and ended with a solo of:

"I'm gonna lay down my sword and shield"....

As a a shocked, but impressed Professor White looked on, and as if rehearsed, everyone finished with a grand:

"Down by the riverside!"

"All aboard," the Conductor shouted, as the engine rumbled like roaring thunder the train jerked, the huge wheels began to slowly turn, a dark cloud of smoke came out of it's top, then it slowly rolled away.

"First stop, Cincinnati!"

"

CHAPTER TWO

In Lebanon, Tennessee, a five-year-old pig-tailed slave girl became impatient as she waited for her mother who was running errands for her Mistress. Little Maggie Porter wandered out of the general store and onto the sidewalk. Though her mother didn't turn around, she felt her leave but wasn't worried because she knew exactly where to find Maggie when the time came.

Once outside, Maggie stood and watched as folks casually passed by on their fancy horses, others in their elegant buggies and still others puttered by in their shabby wagons. Horses' hooves clicked and clopped along as they stirred up clouds of dust. Aromas of fine meats, soups and stews filled the air. The White folks' kids played hide-and-seek and giggled with glee as Maggie slowly passed and wished she could join in, but she knew better than to try. In Tennessee, Coloreds stayed in their place. No looking White folks in the eyes, walk on the other side of the street and stay in a child's place.

Over the sounds of all the busy going-ons, Maggie could faintly hear the choir singing at the church nearby. Her stroll evolved into a brisk walk as she neared the corner in anticipation. The voices became louder, more angelic and clearer as she reached the chapel and took her usual seat on the stoop. The thunder of the massive organ roared. Though she didn't understand their meaning, she knew the words to this song she'd heard them sing on many occasions. Maggie sang along.

"Rock of ages, cleft for me, let me hide myself in thee."

"Them White folks sho' sing pretty songs, momma," she called out as her mother approached and grabbed Maggie by the arm.

"Now come on, Maggie. Come on, child. Every time I turn around, you somewhere lisnin' to the choir. We gotta get back to the fields fo' sun down. We still got cotten-pickin to do. I finished all Miss Eleanor's shopping and we runnin' late. Come on now, Maggie. Come on."

Maggie sprang from the stoop and skipped along to keep up with her mother, continually humming along with the choir.

"One of these days, I'm gon' show folks how to really sing, momma," she vowed. "I'm gon' be pretty, rich and famous, and ain't no White folks gon' be able to tell me what to do. I'm gon' wear fancy clothes and ride in fancy wagons and make everybody call me *Miss, Maggie Porter.* You just wait and see, momma. Just wait and see."

"That's fine, Maggie. But for now, move those little legs of yours and come on chile."

#

In a slave barrack in Tallahatchie, Mississippi, mothers busied themselves cooking, washing clothes and darning socks. Some of their children sat close-by, watching and learning so they would be able to lend a hand when they became of age. The younger kids were running about the room playing tag. Every now and then, one of the mothers would scold them.

"Stop that running."

 Giggles and wonderful aromas filled the air of the otherwise dismal abode; a mere one-room shanty that housed up to three families. Cots and make-shift pads were put down in the evenings for sleeping, and stored away during the day. Milk crates and discarded shipping crates were used as tables and seating. The sun was rapidly setting in the west, prompting one of the mothers to pull the makeshift curtains together as another prepared to light the only oil lamp in the room.

Massa's wife appeared at the creaky wooden door, which was slightly ajar, and momentarily blocked the sun's glare from filling the room. This caught everyone's attention. All activity stopped, including the running children, and the women formed an orderly row, turned their eyes to the floor, and motioned for their children to do the same.

Little Ella Shepard entered the room behind Mistress and ran over to her mother and sheepishly hid behind her apron. She was giggling and twirling one of her braids as the other girls looked on with envy. Ella was being prepped to be a house-nigger, and as such, she was allowed to be inside all day. Unlike them. They were required to pick cotton, which caused their finger-tips great pain and permanent scarring. They were required to lift heavy bags and bales, which caused them severe back problems and deformation of their spines. And they were required to load wagons, only allowed one drink of warm water during the day.

"You this child's mother?" Mistress asked as she reached Sarah and stopped.

"Yes, ma'am, I'se her mammy," Sarah replied, never taking her eyes from the floor.

The other women in the line took a ceremonial step back and listened in, daring to turn their attention away from the dusty floor. Mistress roamed around the room, noticed the steaming pot on the burner and slowly lifted it's lid.

"I see you ladies are making supper for your husbands." She returned the top to the pot and turned her attention back to Sarah. "That's not a turkey bone in that water, is it? You sure there was no meat left on it?"

"Yes, ma'am," Sarah promptly replied. "I made good and sho' there was no meat left on that bone fo' I took it from the big house, ma'am."

The Mistress leered at her, then at the other women in the line. Some dared to turn their heads in another direction, but they dared to look at Mistress. None of them added anything to the conversation, and wisely so.

"Umm, hmm," Massa's wife murmured, doubting if the mother was telling the truth. "And what is this I hear? Something about you being with child?"

A loud, unison gasp filled the room, then a basket of buttons fell to the floor with a shattering repetitiveness. Some of the children giggled, but mothers went scurrying frantically to and fro, rapidly gathering up the mess.

"I ... I ain't quite sho' yet, ma'am," Sarah nervously managed to stutter out.

Though listening to Sarah's explanation, Mistress watched the other women rapidly clean up the mess of buttons.

"I be finding out soon." Sarah shot a glaring stare at Ella, who smiled with great pride and innocence.

"I see," Massa's wife grunted as she slowly sauntered toward the door.

Some of the women thought it best to return to their work. Others mingled into corners and began to quietly gossip.

Massa's wife spoke to them over her shoulder. "Well, you ladies carry on. Your husbands will be in from the fields soon." Then she turned and offered a beautifully-decorated box toward Ella, who quickly ran toward her. As Ella approached, Mistress opened the box and revealed an assortment of fine, fancy chocolates. "We will see you on tomorrow, Ella," she said.

Ella helped herself to one of the chocolates, making the other children's mouths water.

"We'll have some more fun, playing games. Okay?"

"Yes, ma'am, " Ella answered, and teasingly showed her chocolate to the other children who looked on with envy.

Mistress reached for the door as it suddenly opened and the women's husbands were on the other side. Startled, they turned their eyes to the ground and stepped to the side to let her pass. She leered at them, turned her nose up and continued on her way.

"Evnin' ma'am," they said as she passed.

She never looked back but nodded and continued on.

The men began to take off hats, boots, vests and dusty jackets as the women returned to their chores and the children returned to their games. Ella's father approached Sarah and inquired.

"What Massa's wife want?"

The room fell quiet as the others looked on. Some of the women sheltered their children in corners for safety and some of the men drew nearer to hear the mother's response.

"Said, what Massa's wife want?" Mr. Sheppard repeated.

Others in the room shuffled around while keeping a watchful eye. Sarah rubbed her hands against the front of her apron and nervously answered her husband.

"She wanna make sure we got no meat on them turkey bones we boiling."

"Well? Is we?" he asked.

Another mother whispered to him in passing, "No, suh. We took the meat off and dried it months ago."

Some of the women laughed, but others clung to their children and retreated further away from the scene, in expectation of trouble. The men looked to Mr. Sheppard to see what he would do next.

"What else she want?" he demanded.

Just finishing her candy, Ella licked her fingers and innocently answered, "She wanna make sure I wudn't lying to her, daddy."

"Lying bout what?" He turned his attention to Ella.

"Bout the new baby momma's got," Ella said with the proudest smile she could muster up.

Mr. Sheppard turned to his wife, then back to Ella with confusion on this face.

"Ella!" her mother shouted, grabbed the child by the shoulders and had shaken her like a rag doll. "What you don don, child?

Each whining word became a sentence of it's own amidst the shaking as Ella answered. "Nuthin',... mamma....". "We ...was... playn' a... game ...called... 'secrets'... The shaking stopped and the innocence of the child was manifested as she looked into her mother's eyes for

approval. "We plays it everyday." The shaking resumed as Ella resumed. "And… who… got…
the… best… secret… get a sweet treat. "

"No, child!" Sarah screamed in horror.

Mr. Sheppard held his head down in despair and let out a loud sigh.

"I won today, momma. I had the best secret. I won," Ella said with a confused look on
her face.

Gasps from the other mothers filled the room and the other fathers looked to their wives,
then at Ella's father in amazement.

"No, child!" her mother screamed. "What you don don? What you don don?"

Sarah grabbed Ella by the arm and ran toward the door. Mr. Sheppard followed along in
a confused state, and everyone else in the room, adult and child piled out of the barracks after
them.

"Sarah! Sarah!" Mr. Sheppard called out, pleading for his wife to stop, but she continued
to run.

Many others, especially the younger boys, had far-outrun him and reached the bank of the
river no more than a few steps behind the mother and child.

"It's gon be okay, Ella. It's gon be okay," Sarah assured the child. "We'll just say a
prayer and ask God to forgive us, then we'll walk into the river together, and God will be waiting
to take us to the other side. Don't worry. It's gon be okay."

Panting out of breath and relying on his cane and some of the women for his balance,
the Elder finally reached the edge of the river where everyone had gathered.

"What you doin, child? What you doin?" he urgently asked as he approached.

"Oh Elder," Sarah wailed. "Massa's wife been havin' my own child spy on me. They gon' sell me, or even kill me, for sho'."

"Now, now child. Don't you fret," the Elder assured her. "Massa's wife a fine White woman. Even so, God don't need no help from you. When he ready, he gon' send down one of his sweet chariots to carry you, this child, all us home. Yes, Lawd. I can jes see it now. Swing low, sweet chariot. Come on and carry us home."

Someone in the crowd began to moan, then hum, and finally sing:

Swing low, sweet chariot, coming for to carry me home.

Swing low, sweet chariot, coming for to carry me home.

Some of the women in the group helped Ella and Sarah out of the river and they all headed back to their barracks.

#

"Sold!" the Auctioneer yelled as he slammed his gavel down on top of the old decrepit podium which swayed and threatened to topple over. Rising dust from the shuffling of feet floated through the ray of sun coming from the lone window at the top of the barn. The year was 1854. The location: Wilson County, Tennessee. A slave sale.

The room was filled with the organized chaos of White women whispering and gossiping, White men wheeling and dealing, Colored children sniffling and crying, and Colored parents moaning and praying. Buyers on the right, slaves and animals on the left. Keep your mouths shut, your eyes to the ground and your children in line. Those were the rules, and the punishment for breaking them came swift and fierce.

In the midst of it all, a giant of a man stepped up onto the platform with skin darkened by the sun, hair matted from lack of upkeep, eyes swollen shut from his latest beating, body bent over from years of being overworked, and an aura of disappointment and despair. Potential buyers perused their programs to determine if this was the inventory they had come to bid on. The man's wife shook her head in despair, a lone tear descending down the side of her face. She mounted the platform and offered him a drink of water from a ladle.

"You be strong, my beloved husband," she whispered as he held her petite, hard-worked hand between his huge, blistered hands and thirstily drank. Their eyes briefly met.

"Don't you let them break you, Walter. I'm gon' remember you as the strong, loving man who did his best to protect his wife and children. I'm gon' always remember your gentle touch. You are my warrior, my prince, my reason to press on. You stay strong my brave soldier. You stay strong. One day weez gon' be free. I promise to look for you. Until we meet again, my sweet love."

A tear rolled down his cheek as he turned his face to the ground, and she returned to her place before being noticed.

Just then, a befuddled mother with a toddler on her hip and eight other children in tow, entered the barn and cautiously looked around before proceeding.

"Come on, yungins. Stay together. Come on, now," she instructed.

"What about this fine, strong one?" the Auctioneer started up, referring to the man on the platform. "Stands at least 6 feet and looks as though he's been fed quite well…for a slave. Do I hear a bid?"

The befuddled mother slowly ushered her children past the giant-sized man and they all took their place in line, next to be sold.

"I'll give you no more than $200 for him," someone yelled from the rear of the room, and everyone laughed.

"Throw in two oxen and I'll take them all for $500!" a more serious bidder called out.

"Sold, to the fine gentleman from Nashville!" the Auctioneer proudly announced as he slammed the gavel on top of the podium, causing the befuddled woman and all 9 children to startle.

The huge man descended from the platform and was dragged away by the heavy chains about his body. The clanking of the chains and shackles rang in his wife's ears and she cupped them with her hands. Finally, she let out a shrill scream, then suddenly regained her composure and sadly walked away. The befuddled mother and her clan moved up to the front of the line.

"I ain't goin, momma," the eldest boy protested. "Ain't being sold like some kinda animal. Here they don' freed slaves in the North. Should just make a run for it. Hear they's got peoples who help you along the way. Some kind of railroad."

"Shish that kind of crazy talk, son!" the mother sternly warned. She attempted to grab him by the arm, but he yanked away from her grip. "You been man of this family since yo' pappy left, but I ain't lisnin' to none of that *free slave* mess. You shut yo' mouth, and just do what these White folks say, then maybe…just maybe, we can stay **together**!" she scolded as she helped the smaller children onto the platform.

The auctioneer yelled to her from behind his podium, "Where's these kids pappy?"

Making sure to keep her eyes to the floor and motioning for her children to do the same, the mother replied, "Don't know, suh. Either run off or was sold fo' this one here - Thomas, was born." She moved the child from one hip to the other as she continued. "Ain't seen 'em since, suh."

"Humph," the Auctioneer grunted under his breath, then looked at them with disgust. "Well, let's see what we can do with the bunch of ya."

"I'ze be very grateful if you could sell us all together, suh. Very grateful," the mother pleaded, never taking her eyes from the floor.

"Don't sass me, gal. Like I said, we will see what we can do," he snapped.

"Get your brothers and sisters, son," the mother pleaded. "Let's stay together, now."

"What do I hear for this fine family of one, two, three, four, five, six, seven, eight, nine," he pointed at each child as he counted. " A mammy with nine yungins! The oldest is almost a man. What do I hear for the whole bunch of 'em? Let's start the bidding off at $900. We'll throw the little one in for free. Surely they're good for a full day's work. You could clear your fields in half the time. Do I hear $850 for 'em? Surely they are worth $850."

After much murmuring, someone finally called out, "I'll take the two eldest boys for $500."

The mother began to pray quietly under her breath, "Please, Lord. I'm trying to keep my family together. Please let somebody take all us."

"I will take all of them for $800," someone else yelled out from the crowd.

"Thank you, Lord. Thank you," the mother whispered.

"Sold to the fine gentleman from Alabama! Now get 'em outta here. The whole bunch of 'em," the Auctioneer demanded and slammed his gavel on top of the podium.

"All except that baby," the buyer added as he spun around. "Won't do me no good. Can't work no fields." Then he merely turned and began to walk away.

Before she realized it, the mother looked up and called out, "Oh, please suh. "Please, don't make me leave my child!"

Just then, the buyer's daughter had joined him and looked on in despair.

"Come along, my dear daughter. You've seen enough of this," he said, and interlocked her arm under his. He then returned his attention to the mother, who held on to her child for dear life. The eldest son and the others had already started to head toward the wagon without protest. "Can't do nothing with a baby, gal! Now, leave it behind and get on the wagon," the buyer demanded, then nodded to his Foreman as he and his daughter continued to walk away.

"Please, massa. Please don't make me leave my child!" the mother called after him. "I'll do whatever you say. I'll work your fields, tend to your young…."

"Let go of this yungin before I have to lash you, woman," the foreman warned as he stepped in and took hold of the child's arm.

"No," the mother asserted, tears streaming down her face. "You gon' have to kill me. I ain't leaving my child", she declared. "Suh, please!" she called out to the buyer, but he and his daughter continued to walk away. "I'll pray for your sick and tend to your dying. Please, suh, don't make me leave my baby!" she screamed at the top of her voice.

The first lash the foreman delivered sent her to the floor, cradling her child in her arms as she fell. She rolled over on top of him to protect him from the next lash, which she knew was sure to follow. The buyer's daughter shivered. The mother's children never looked back, but scurried even faster to get on the wagon awaiting them. The father and his daughter continued on their way as they heard the second lash, which cut her clear across the back and ripped her already-tattered dress. The mother let out a long, howling scream, and the buyer's daughter suddenly stopped, ran back and called out to her father as she reached the mother's side.

"Father, please. Can't you see this mother's pain? I'll take care of the child."

"Why, what would you do with a Colored child, my sweetest?" the father scoffed.

The distraught mother pulled herself up and checked her child for injury. Then, in a bold move, she stared both the buyer and his daughter in the eye in a silent plea; tears mixed with blood streaming down her cheek.

"Well, I can practice being a mother," the daughter proudly announced. "Don't forget. I am about to become a wife soon," she reminded her father.

Reluctantly, the father conceded. "Very well. Come along. But I warn you. This child will *not* interfere with his mother's work."

"I understand. Thank you, father," she called to him as he continued on his way, then returned her attention to the waiting mother. "What is this child's name?" she softly asked while receiving the child from the grateful mother.

"Thomas. Thomas Rutling, ma'am. Thank you, ma'am. God bless you all yo' days. Thank you."

The befuddled mother began to walk along with the buyer's daughter when she was suddenly grabbed by each arm by two official-looking White men who steered her body in a different direction from that of the buyer's daughter . She became frightened and her eyes widened as she frantically turned her head in all directions, looking to see where her children were. "What ya'll doing? My children! What you doin!" she protested.

The buyer's daughter went on her way as the mother was dragged off kicking and screaming. Her children looked on in tears; including Thomas.

CHAPTER THREE

Days later when the train started to slow, then finally stopped, the students had arrived at

Fountain Square. What was once a butcher's market that had recently been turned into town

square just that year, Fountain Square was now center of Cincinnati. In 1847, Levi Coffin, a

businessman, humanitarian, and American Quaker made the Cincinnati area the center of his

anti-slavery efforts. He was an abolitionist, and most importantly, an active leader in the

Underground Railroad in Indiana and Ohio. His home in Fountain City, Indiana was often called

the "Grand Central Station" of the Underground Railroad, and he was given the unofficial title of

"President of the Underground Railroad." It is estimated that 3,000 fugitive slaves passed

through his care.

Many of the slaves passing through this area often ran into and spoke with Harriet
Beecher Stowe, author of "Uncle Tom's Cabin". Stowe lived in Cincinnati for a time and based
her novel on stories the escaped slaves told as they passed through.

Everyone grabbed their bags and gathered with great anticipation in an area Mrs. Bennett
directed them to. After a short while, a cloaked stranger showed up and took Professor White to
the side. The two spoke briefly as Frederick Loudin lurked in the wings.

\#

Frederick Jeremiah Loudin was born to free parents on January 1,1836 in Charlestown, Ohio. In
a strategic move, his parents relocated to Burlington, Vermont where they supported Hiram
College, a private Liberal Arts college founded in 1850 under the name of the Western Reserve
Eclectic Institute. Over the years, thinking they were securing Frederick's future acceptance and
enrollment at the institution, Loudin's family made regular financial contributions to them.
When time came for Frederick to enroll, their donations had not, indeed, secured Loudin's
acceptance. They, therefore, uprooted their family and moved back to Ohio to become farmers.

Segregation was legal at the time, but since he was born free, Loudin's parents boldly
enrolled him in public school with the White kids. Ridiculed and bullied on his first day of
school, Loudin experienced his first treatment of racism.

"What are you doing here, Nigger? This is a White school," one of the students had
yelled at him across the lawn.

"Yeah. Get off of our campus, Nigger. You are not wanted here," another student yelled
out.

Though Frederick learned to ignore them, every day he was met with threat after threat until one day, as he made his way through the gauntlet of ridicule, someone threw a rock and struck him in the head, just above the eye. Frederick dropped his books when he felt the stream of blood begin to roll down his face. He covered his eye with his handkerchief and ran all the way home. His mother was appalled to see her son in such a bloody mess. She cleaned him up and consoled him until he calmed down and thereafter refused to deal with the continued racial discrimination at the schools in the area. Thereafter, she took her children to the town of Ravenna, Ohio to be educated.

Absent the overt racism, Loudin became a very strong student in Ravenna, excelled in his studies, and was once placed in a coveted seat in class that was reserved for high-achievers. When the White parents heard of this, many of them pulled their kids out of the school, rather than have them shown up by a Colored kid. They preferred the seat be filled by a student based on his race, rather than his merit.

The next time discrimination surfaced it's ugly head, Loudin was in his late teens and had been fortunate to begin an apprenticeship with a local printer as a Compositor. One of the local abolitionist papers heard about how dependable and efficient he was, and the Editor summoned Frederick to his office. He wore his best pair of slacks and a clean, white shirt, then went to speak with the Editor.

"Good day, Sir," Frederick said with a small tilt of his head as he entered the office.

The Editor looked up from his work. "Frederick. Please have a seat," he motioned to a chair across from him. "Thank you for being on time. That shows great professionalism on your part."

Loudin took a seat as asked. "Thank you, Sir. I've been told that you're looking to fill a very important position on your staff. I'm anxious to hear your proposal."

"Yes. We're looking for someone to take over the Literary Department here, and thought you might make a good fit."

Frederick searched for the right words, then spoke. "It sounds like a very impressive position, Sir, and I'm honored that you are offering me such a fine opportunity. However, I must admit I don't know the first thing about running a department."

"That's not a problem, Frederick. You see…" he paced the room as he lit his pipe and blew an impressive ring of smoke from his mouth. "It's not always *what* you know Frederick."

"Excuse me, Sir?" Frederick asked, clearly confused.

The Editor faced him. "Sometimes it's more of *who* you know, than it is of *what* you know. If you know the right people, you can learn what you need to know from them."

Loudin hesitated as he contemplated the Editor's remarks. "If I may be honest, Sir."

"Please do." The Editor leaned forward and waited for Frederick to explain his position.

"I don't agree with your views on many points regarding the treatment of the newly-freed slaves, so I don't know if I would be as effective a candidate as the position requires."

The Editor was taken aback by Frederick's position. He had expected him to immediately jump at the chance to fill such an important position.

"What are you saying, Frederick? Certainly, you are not considering passing up such a fine opportunity?"

"Unfortunately, Sir, I must. I do appreciate the consideration, however," he added as he stood to his feet.

"I'm very sorry to hear that, Frederick. However, I respect your decision and appreciate your stopping by."

"Thank you, Sir. I'll be on my way. Good day to you," he said as he stood, turned and left.

Loudin remained a Compositor and set out to gain new business for his benefactor. He set up appointment after appointment with the town's printers and publishers, but after several rejections he realized the White printers were refusing to do business with him because he was Colored. As a result, a discouraged Loudin eventually gave up printing, altogether.

#

"Thank you for assisting us," Professor White whispered as he shook the cloaked stranger's hand. Still lurking in the shadows, Frederick Loudin noticed the brief exchange of cash the Professor slipped to the stranger.

"Let's move hastily," the stranger said, and Professor White nodded to Pastor and Mrs. Bennett, who directed the students to follow her.

"Hurry along, students. Hurry along," Mrs. Bennett encouraged them.

Under the cover of darkness, they were clandestinely ushered to the rear of a near-by building where they took several stairs to a lower level. Once there, in the mildew-infested basement they found make-shift cots placed in two rows. A wall of sheets hung between the rows to separate the boys' side from the girls' side. A more cozier area in a corner of the room was set up for Pastor and Mrs. Bennett.

"Put your things underneath the cots, children," Mrs. Bennett instructed in a hushed tone. "Pastor Bennett will arrive shortly to go over your bible studies and to have the evening prayer.

Thereafter, we will have something to eat, then everyone will retire for the evening. Are there any questions?" she asked as she looked around the room at nine proud, yet afraid, young people.

No one had any questions. Therefore, Mrs. Bennett turned to leave as the students began to put their belongings away as instructed. All, except Maggie Porter.

"This is where they expect us to lodge?" Maggie questioned.

Mrs. Bennett overheard and turned back around. She slowly scanned the room toward the location she believed the voice originated. The girls were standing erect with their arms to their sides. All except Maggie, who stood with her arms folded across her chest. Mrs. Bennett approached her.

"Excuse me," she apologized. "Your name is?"

"My name is Miss, Maggie Porter," Maggie smarted.

"Well, Miss, Maggie Porter, if you want to remain part of this troupe, you will have to mind your manners. Is that clear?"

Before she realized it, Maggie had turned her eyes to the floor and was humbly apologizing. "I'm sorry, ma'am. You're right. I should just be grateful to be along."

"That's better," Mrs Bennett said, then turned and left the room.

All of the other students looked at one another in shock. Maggie had finally met her match.

CHAPTER FOUR

"Please come in," Dean Cravath, one of the founders of the newly-formed Fisk Free-Colored School called out from within his office.

Before entering the room, Thomas Rutling, now a pre-teen, straightened his bow tie and brushed off his jacket. The Dean looked over the rim of his glasses as Thomas entered. Then he arose from his huge, leather chair and placed both fists on his hips as he received his guest.

"Come on in, young man. Have a seat," he motioned. "Have a seat."

Thomas walked over to an oak bench and sat down.

"And you are?" The Dean returned to his dusty, leather chair.

"My name is Thomas. Thomas Rutling from Wilson County, Tennessee, Sir."

The Dean touched his chin and looked to the ceiling.

"About 20 miles from Nashville, Sir," Thomas clarified.

"I see. I don't think I've ever had the opportunity to visit that area of Tennessee. Good to make your acquaintance, young man. How might we help you today?"

Thomas straightened his posture on the hard bench, then continued.

"Sir, I was youngest of nine children and born into slavery. At the young age of 3, during a slave sale, my master's daughter bargained with her father for my life so that I could remain with my mother. Therefore, I was reared by my master's daughter, and when she married and moved to her own plantation, she took two of my siblings and myself with her."

"What a lovely gesture," the Dean agreed.

"Unfortunately, our plantation was raided in 1864, so in 1865 my brother and I left for Nashville. There we found, yet, another sister who taught me to read and write."

"I see," the Dean nodded.

"Because I could read and write, I was fortunate enough to secure a position as a Surgeon's Assistant whose associate kindly provided me with a letter of recommendation to attend this fine institution for learning."

Thomas reached into his nap sack and retrieved a piece of parchment paper. "I have my tuition right here." He stood and pulled some bills out of his pants pocket. "The entire six dollars, Sir," Thomas proudly announced as he offered the money and the paperwork to the Dean.

"I see, I see," the Dean repeated as he accepted the bills and the papers. He put the bills in a small, black cash box on his desk, then briefly perused the papers.

He spoke as he read. "You would, in fact, be one of our first students here at the American Missionary Association's Fisk Free-Colored School, young man. Let's see what we have here."

After looking at the papers briefly, he looked up at Thomas in shock. "It says here that you are only 14 years old!"

"Yes, Sir."

"I must say, you do come highly recommended by the Surgeon and his associate...." His eyes moved to the bottom of the written communication, in search of the writer's signature, then widened as he read it aloud, "the Honorable General Clinton B. Fisk, himself." He paused briefly, then read on. "It says here that you proved to be an excellent Assistant to the Surgeon, and he thinks you might benefit even further from what we have to offer here at the university."

The Dean sat the papers down, stood and wandered over to the window where he looked out over the many tents that made up the campus' infrastructure. He sighed heavily.

"Though it previously served as barracks for the Union Army, it's turning out to be a fine campus. The tent we are standing in was the former military hospital barracks."

'Yes, Sir, it is a very fine campus, from what I've seen so far. I look forward to getting started right away. Might I be assisting one of the surgeons here? Or maybe one of the Professors?"

"Now, let's not get too hasty, young man."

The Dean returned to his chair and slowly sat down. "You will have to earn your keep by waiting tables in the faculty lounge. Why don't you make your way over there and get acquainted with the staff? Welcome to the Fisk Free-Colored School. That will be all."

Though disappointed, Thomas stood and gathered his things. "Thank you, Sir. I'll make my way over there now, if you will head me in the right direction."

"Just follow your nose, young man. Just follow your nose."

They both laughed and Thomas went on his way.

When he was sure he was out of ear's reach of the Dean, he muttered to himself, "Waiting tables in the faculty lounge?" He shrugged his shoulders and began to sing as he went in search of the faculty lounge:

"I come from Alabama with my banjo on my knee,

I'm going to Louisiana, my true love for to see.

It rained all night the day I left, the weather it was dry,

The sun so hot I froze to death, Susanna, don't you cry.#

Professor George White came around the corner just as Thomas reached it and heard him end the song.

"Oh, Susana, don't you cry for me,

I come from Alabama with my banjo on my knee."

"You seem to have quite a promising voice, young man," George White complimented as Thomas passed him. "Do come see me in the music room when you get settled."

Thomas turned and continued walking backwards as he called to White. "Been singing all my life, Sir. And the music room would be located where?"

"Not quite sure yet. Better yet, I will find you. How is that?" George White chuckled.

"That is just fine with me," Thomas called back, then continued on his way as George White entered the Dean's office.

"Mr White. So good to see you again." The Dean stood and extended his hand. "I had no idea you were in the area. Last I heard, you were in Chattanooga. To what do we owe the pleasure of your visit today?"

The two men shook hands, then the Dean motioned for White to have a seat in one of the chairs near his desk.

"Well, Sir," White started as he sat. "Since leaving the Army, I joined the Freedmen's Bureau in Nashville. Shameful, but the city is crowded with impoverished former slaves."

"Yes, it is, indeed," the Dean agreed.

"I have come to offer my services to this great institution, the Fisk Free-Colored school. I thought, maybe, I could teach music."

The Dean chuckled briefly. "I beg your pardon, Mr. White," he hesitated. "Liberal Arts have never been offered to Coloreds, and I don't know if we want to be the first to offer it."

George White repositioned himself in the seat. "I'm aware of that, Sir. I thought, maybe it is time we rectify that. What harm could it do? In addition, what if I also teach penmanship?"

The Dean stood and walked over to the make-shift window where he looked over the campus. "I see, I see." He rubbed his chin in contemplation. "Well, I'm sure the Coloreds need the penmanship. However, I doubt if any of them would be interested in singing in a choir. They only know the songs of their ancestors, and no one wants to hear that." He turned and faced White before continuing. "Furthermore, there is no money in the budget to pay a music teacher. So, frankly, I don't see how I can be of any assistance to you at this time, Mr. White."

"Respectfully, Sir," George White stood. "I'm prepared to offer my services on a voluntary basis."

"Oh, I see," the Dean said with raised eyebrows, then stood and extended a hand to White. "Well, under those circumstances, how could we possibly say 'no'?" He beamed as he shook George White's hand.

"Very well. I'll seek out a work area and get started right away. That young man who was just leaving seemed to have quite a voice. Where might I find him?"

The Dean walked Professor White to the door. "Why, you can find Mr. Rutling in the faculty lounge; waiting tables."

"Very well. I will surely keep you informed of my progress. Thank you, Sir, for the opportunity."

As the two men reached the door, someone knocked from the other side.

"Come in, come in," the Dean called out. "Good day to you, Mr. White," he added, turned and returned to his large, leather chair.

When he looked up, a twelve-year-old colored girl slowly sauntered into the room, stuck her nose up in the air and did a slow, 180 degree turn as she took in the decor. The Dean nervously shuffled the papers on his desk.

"Good day, kind Sir. My name is Maggie. Miss, Maggie Porter." Though she extended a gloved hand, the Dean merely stood and acknowledged her presence. "I was told I might be able to enroll into this fine teaching establishment for Coloreds," she continued.

The Dean directed her attention to an empty chair and handed her several sheets of paper.

"Very well, very well. Just fill out these few papers, then return them to me. You do know how to read and write, don't you?"

"Why, of course I do, Sir."

"Very well. Then, I will leave you to that. I shall return shortly."

When he left the room, Maggie rolled her eyes around in her head and mocked him, "*You do know how to read and write, don't you?* I probably read *and* write better than he does. Hmph."

CHAPTER FIVE

Soon after the near-drowning incident, Ella Sheppard's father was down trodden and troubled at

heart, as the near-tragic incident had left him fearing for his wife's sanity and his daughter's

safety. One Sunday afternoon, once church services were over, Mr. Sheppard decided to go to

his master to petition him for the lives of his wife and daughter. Wearing his best Sunday suit of

burlap pants and a cotton shirt, he used a long piece of twine as a make-shift belt. He brushed

his hair back, shined up his dusty boots and chewed on a cinnamon stick to freshen his breath.

He then walked up to the big house, climbed the twenty or so steps at the front of the house,

walked through the courtyard, then finally arrived at the huge, oak front doors and knocked.

After what seemed like forever, one side of the massive door opened ever so slightly, and Sadie,

the head house nigger stood behind the door and peeked around to see who was on the other side.

"Good afternoon." She squinted as she looked. "Aint you that nigger whose wife is

crazy and almost killed your daughter? What you doing knocking on master's door for? You

crazy, too?" she squinted even harder.

"No, ma'am. I aint crazy," he shamefully answered. "Desperate, maybe,. But not crazy. I need to see massa."

"Bout what?"

"Sadie!" Massa called out as he approached. "What did I tell you about questioning my slaves? Back to your post, woman."

Sadie did as told, turned and left the two men alone. Massa opened the door wider and stepped out onto the porch. Mr. Sheppard stepped back, as not to be rude. He removed his hat and nervously twirled it around in his hand. He kept his eyes to the ground.

"Why are you on my porch?" Massa barked at him.

"Good afternoon, Sir. I come to ask permission to purchase my wife, Sarah, and my daughter, Ella, and take them to Nashville, Sir."

"Why would I let you do that?" Massa demanded to know.

"My wife, Sir. My wife ain't right in the head."

"Oh, I see," Massa remembered. "You are the nigger whose wife almost drowned your daughter. I can see why you would want to take your daughter, but what would you do with your wife? You can't afford to get her the help she needs."

"My wife ain't crazy. She was just scared. She just need to be away from here. Please, Sir. Have mercy on me."

"How much money you got?" Massa abruptly asked.

"I aint got but $350, Sir. I know it aint much, but it's all I got."

"Give me the money," Massa demanded.

Mr. Sheppard reached into the pocket of his pants and pulled the money out, which he anxiously offered to Massa. He was suddenly overcome with a feeling of hope as Massa retrieved a handkerchief from his pocket and motioned for Mr. Sheppard to put the money into the hankie, which he did.

"You can take your daughter, but your wife stays," he emphatically stated.

Before Mr. Sheppard could say anything else, Massa had turned and walked away.

Mr. Sheppard had left well enough alone, returned to the slave barracks and found his wife sitting by the fire, holding Ella, and singing "Swing Low, Sweet Chariot". He approached carefully and cautiously as not to frighten her. Ella had just dozed off, so he took her from her mother and gently laid her in bed. Then, he pulled a knitted shawl from a nail on the wall and picked up an oil lamp. He folded the shawl over his arm and motioned for his wife to head toward the door.

"It's a beautiful moon tonight, Sarah. Why don't we go for a walk in the moonlight?" he whispered.

Sarah looked up at him and smiled. "That sounds like a lovely idea, dear."

She allowed him to wrap the shawl around her shoulders and they walked through the door and out into the darkness. Mr. Sheppard closed the door behind them, and as he held the lantern in one hand so that it would light their way, he used his other hand to hold his wife's arm as she descended the two steps down to the dusty ground.

"Watch your step, dear," he warned.

The two of them walked along the dusty path, arm in arm. They smelled the wood burning in the fireplace at the big house, mixed with the fragrance of the numerous jasmine trees. The beaming moon helped light their way.

"I'm so sorry, dear," Sarah said, finally breaking the silence as she stopped walking and turned to face him. "I don't know what came over me." She raised both hands to her temples and continued. "I was so afraid, I didn't know what I was doing." She looked deep into his eyes as tears began to well up in the corners of her eyes. "Can you ever forgive me?"

"You fret not, my dear wife," he answered and took her in his arms. "You fret not. I forgive you, Sarah."

He motioned for her to sit on the tree stump nearby, then he adjusted the shawl about her shoulders. They sat in silence for a moment. An owl in the distance softly hooted his rhythmic night melody.

"I need you to be strong, though, Sarah. I got something I need to tell you."

He took her small hands into his large, overworked hands and held on tight.

"What is it, dear?"

"I went to see Massa today."

"What you do that for?" Sarah snatched her hands away and fear came over her.

"I asked to purchase you and Ella, so we can get outta here."

Sarah's eyes lit up at this wonderful news, and she fell into his arms and exhaled a breath she had been holding forever.

"Thank God," she cried. "Thank God."

"Hold on, Sarah," he cautioned as he stood up. "Let me finish."

He took a step back and looked into her eyes as she stood to face him.

"What he say?" Sarah asked with hope.

"Massa said I can buy Ella, but he won't let me buy you."

The tears that had welled up in her eyes now began to fall as his words cut her deep. She was quiet for a long time, then she sat back down.

"You gon' take my child from me?"

"Don't look at it as taking her from you. I'm trying to give her a chance at freedom. A chance to live a child's life. A chance to grow up feeling safe, and maybe go to school. Don't you want the same thing for her; freedom?"

They gazed at the moon and watched the twinkling of the stars as the incessant chirping of crickets and frogs' croaks broke the silence. A coyote howled in the distance.

"Yes, dear. I know you right," Sarah finally agreed as she hung her head. "It's for the best, even though it's gon' break my heart. But you take our precious daughter to freedom. I'll be fine. I'll be just fine."

Mr. Sheppard put his arms around his distraught wife and held her close and tight, and let her cry until she ran out of tears.

Soon-after, Mr. Sheppard and Ella left a sad and depressed Sarah at massa's plantation and headed for Nashville where he started his own business. However, when his business failed, creditors threatened to seize his new wife in lieu of payment. As a result, and in fear, he took his family and fled to Cincinnati.

Only a few year laters, on his death bed Mr. Sheppard had called Ella into his room, and in between coughing fits, had visited with her.

"Oh, father," Ella had wailed. "What will I ever do without you?"

"You'll be fine, my sweet daughter. Just remember that you are better than no one, but as good as anyone."

Ella could hear the congestion rattling around in his chest, and he was wheezing as he spoke in a near-whisper.

"Make me and your mother proud by minding your manners and keeping up with your studies. Keep yourself clean so that you can find yourself a good, God-fearing man when you finish your education." After he finished a coughing spell, he continued. "Take care of your step-mother. Do as she says. She only has your best interest at heart. And be kind to your step-sister. You both have the same blood running through your veins. Never forget that blood is thicker than water." He struggled to reach over to his night stand, so Ella assisted him by opening the drawer, from which he retrieved a bible. He opened the bible and flipped through a few pages until he found what he was looking for. "Here. You take this," he instructed Ella, and handed her a folded sheet of paper which she opened and read as he went into another coughing spell. "Use that to find your mother."

Ella read the official-looking document out loud:

"Notice"

By virtue of a deed of trust, executed by Georgia R. Wallace to the subscriber, bearing date the 5th day of November, 1822 and recorded in the county court of Tallahatchie, Mississippi, to secure the payment of a certain sum of money therein mentioned, I shall on the 20th day of November next, at the tavern of L.P. Smith, in Tallahatchie sell to the highest bidder, for cash, a Negro Slave, named Sarah Hannah Sheppard, mentioned in said deed, now in

possession of said Wallace. Such title will be made as is vested in the subscriber, Walter T.

Clark. October 1, 1822.

As tears welled up in her eyes, Ella carefully refolded the note and put it in her pocket.

"Thank you, father. I promise to do my best; both in school and in finding my mother. I

will miss you, father. Please don't go. What will I ever do without you?" she sobbed.

"You'll be fine, Ella. Use those voice and piano classes and make something of yourself.

Try to get yourself into a school. Maybe that Fisk Free-Colored school down in Nashville.

You'll be just fine."

When he went into, yet, another coughing spell, Ella burst into tears and laid her head on

his chest. She began to hum "Swing Low, Sweet Chariot" as her father took his last breath,

slowly closed his eyes and died. Ella screamed in agony, and her step-mother came into the

room and consoled her.

#

"Walk with me, Lord, walk with me,

Walk with me, Lord, walk with me,

While I'm on this tedious journey, Lord

Walk with me, Lord, walk with me."

Just a few short weeks later, Ella Sheppard sang while sitting atop a crate on a street

corner in Gallatin, Tennessee. Her angelic soprano voice melodiously filled the air. Ella's father

had told her about the new, free-colored school that had just opened in Nashville, and she was determined to raise the $6 she needed to enroll. So, as she sang her way from Cincinnati to Nashville, she pan-handled to raise her tuition.

> *"Hold my hand, Lord, Hold my hand,*
>
> *Hold my hand, Lord, Hold my hand,*
>
> *While I'm on this tedious journey, Lord*
>
> *Hold my hand, Lord, Hold my hand."*

Some passer-bys would stop and listen, some would reward her with broad smiles, some with assuring nods of the head. Every now and then, some would even put a few coins in her cup.

This particular day, two elderly, Colored ladies rapidly approached; clearly with an end destination in mind. Ella was sure they had no time to stop and no money to give. But, given the late hour, the women fooled her, stopped and showed concern. The short one had wiry hair hidden under a faded, blue hat, and had to be no taller than Ella; even with her heels on. The other lady was taller and quite large around the middle. Her hair was thicker and wavier than the short lady, and she had red freckles covering both cheeks. She wobbled back and forth as she struggled to get along. They both were wearing gloves that appeared to have once been White, knitted shawls, printed dresses, a simple strand of pearls, and they both smelled of liniment.

"My sweet child. What you doin' out here all alone this time of night? You just a baby. Where yo' folks?" the thoughtful, wiry-haired woman asked.

The sun was just beginning to set and shop owners began to lock up their businesses. The church bells began to toll, passer-bys began to hurry along to get out of the cover of darkness, and the town began to turn in for the night. Ella rose from the crate.

""I'm already 15, ma'am. I hear my mother is still in Mississippi, forced to remain a slave. My father gave me a copy of a notice of intent to assist in finding her."

Ella bent down and removed the warm, burlap blanket she'd been sitting on from the top of the crate. It was a special blanket she took every where she went because her mother had made it for her when she was a child. She carefully folded the blanket and put it in her shoulder bag. "My father died of cholera just a few, short weeks ago. Started singing to support myself and my step mother."

"What's your name, gal?" the obese woman asked.

"Ella. Ella Sheppard." Ella nodded her head at the two ladies, closed the large book that held the sheet music she had been singing from and placed it inside the bag, along with the blanket. She removed her silk scarf from the bag before closing it.

"I must say, Ella Sheppard. You got the prettiest voice I ever heard. I thought I was listening to an angel," the thoughtful woman laughed.

""Thank you, ma'am." Ella tied her scarf about her head, then used her hands to smooth her dress.

"Where you from? What you doin' here?" Nosy asked.

Ella began to slowly stroll away, and the two women joined her as she continued her story. "I was born in Mississippi; a slave girl. My daddy purchased me for $350, but the White folks wouldn't let him purchase my real mama, because she tried to drown me when I was six years old."

The two ladies stopped, clutched their pearls and leaned back in shock with their mouths gaped open and their eyes widened as wide as they could go.

"So, my daddy found hisself a new wife and bought her for $1,300," Ella continued.

"Shut yo' mouth," Thoughtful responded.

"My daddy was a smart, proud man. Had his own business in Nashville. Don't know why he suddenly moved us to Cincinnati. I wore pretty dresses, went to school, I even took singing and piano lessons."

"Singing *and* piano. Your daddy must have been a smart *and* rich man," Nosy smarted.

"Sure did. I was only allowed to come at night," Ella whispered. "And I had to enter through the back door, but I learned how to play and sing as good as anybody."

"So, how did you end up here, in Gallatin, Tennessee?" Nosy inquired.

"Came here to help out with the newly-freed slaves. Thought I would be able to help out teaching, but I found out real soon that nobody respects a 15-year-old. So I've decided to go to the new Colored school in Nashville as soon as I save up the tuition."

"You mean the American Missionary Association school; the Fisk Free-Colored school?" Thoughtful confirmed.

"That's the one. I hear they let Coloreds actually take liberal arts classes there."

"Yes, I believe I heard something about that. They say the Western Freedmen's Bureau joined up with the American Missionary Association and opened several institutions of learning for newly-freed slaves," Nosy boasted, then whispered to Ella, "all White folks ain't bad White folks."

All three of them laughed.

"Been saving up for five months, now," Ella proudly announced.

"How much you got saved?" Nosy pried.

"You so nosy," Thoughtful scoffed.

"I got $5.00," Ella whispered.

"Shut yo' mouth! How much it cost?" Thoughtful asked.

"Now look who's being nosy," Nosy snapped.

Ella stopped walking, so the ladies did the same.

"It's quite expensive," she assured them. "I hear it's $6.00. That will get me in and cover at least 3 weeks' schooling."

"That *is* quite expensive," Thoughtful agreed as she fidgeted with a small, satin pouch she had taken from somewhere inside her jacket pocket, opened it and retrieved some coins. "What you plan to do after that?"

"Oh, I think I'll put those piano lessons to work and teach other students to play. Who knows? I might even become a teacher, myself," Ella proudly announced.

Nosy merely looked the other way and mumbled to herself, " This child got big dreams. Ain't no such thing as a Colored teacher."

"Well, here you go, dear," Thoughtful said as she dropped some coins into Ella's can. "Now, it's getting late. You get yourself someplace safe for the evening. Good luck at Fisk Free-Colored school. I'm sure you'll do just fine."

Ella's eyes lit up in glee as she heard the coins clang together as they dropped.

"Thank you so much."

Thoughtful looked over at Nosy, who was clutching her pocketbook close to her chest. Nosy stared back at her, puzzled.

"Give the girl some money," Thoughtful demanded.

"I ain't got no money," Nosy lied as she turned away.

"You got money. Give the girl something. Don't be so stingy. Give the girl something."

Nosy reluctantly looked down into her pocketbook, and Thoughtful also attempted to look.

"Don't be in my business," Nosy warned as she came out with a few coins and dropped them into Ella's tin can.

The two women continued on their way, leaving Ella on her own.

"You so stingy," Thoughtful scolded as they walked away.

"And you so nosy," Nosy shot back.

"Stingy thing."

"Nosy thing."

Neither of them heard Ella as she called to them, "I promise to do my best. Come on, Jesus. Let's go. Enough walking. RUN with me to school!"

CHAPTER SIX

On June 19, 1866 somewhere down south in Texas, the day had started like any other. They had

risen before the sun and said their morning prayers. They thanked God for a new day, the gift of

life, their health, their children and their slave masters. Then they asked God to save them from

the toils of their new day, the curse of being born into a slave life, from the rapid deterioration of

their health, the unpredictable futures of their children, and their slave masters.

The men alternated turns at the face bowl and the out-house while the women prepared

breakfast of freshly-laid eggs, scrapple and pan-fried corn cakes. The aroma of the sizzling

scrapple aroused the children awake, and they rose with huge yawns, wiping sleep from their

eyes. Everyone had a chore and stuck to it, which greatly helped to keep the barracks running in

good order. Two mothers were responsible for all diapering and feeding duties of the babies, two

mothers tended to the older girls, and two of the older boys tended to the younger boys. Three mothers tended to the laundry duties, and all the able-bodied fathers and the older boys prepared to go to the fields to pick cotton from sun-up to sundown.

At 6:00 a.m., sharp, the work wagon arrived. Once all had boarded and settled down, the horses were commanded to proceed. The wagon jerked and the huge, wooden wheels began to slowly turn. They rode in silence and mentally prepared themselves for a long, work-filled day. When they arrived to the work site, they all piled out and stood in two rows; young men in the front line and the elders in the back line. The foreman assigned them to sections of the cotton field, and they each grabbed a burlap bag and went their separate ways.

Shortly after they began to pick, they heard the clip-clop of an approaching horse. Some continued to pick, but others looked up and were amazed to see a Colored man they had never seen in the area before, riding the horse. A rare and suspicious sight, indeed.

"Must be a free niggah from the north," one of them commented under his breath, but no one responded. They continued to pick until their morning water break. As they gathered around the water wagon, they heard the clip-clop of another horse approaching. They took turns passing the ladle as they watched another Colored man pass by and wave to them as if he had not a care in the world. Even stranger than the previous man, this man had a rickety wagon hitched to the back of his horse, and what looked like all of his worldly possessions loaded on the wagon, which made it lean to the side.

"Why ya'll still workin'?" he called to them as he smiled, waved and rode by.

"What's going on?" one of the young men asked quietly as he looked around to make sure the foreman was not watching.

"Don't pay him no mind," one of the older men answered. "Probably just some crazy niggah on his way to slaughter when they catch up with him. Let's get back to work."

They returned to the fields and continued their work. As the day progressed, some of their finger tips began to bleed and grow blisters. Knowing there was nothing they could do about it until the noon break, they dared to complain and continued their work in silence. One of the elders noticed an aloe bush nearby, pulled his make-shift knife from his pocket and snipped off a small piece of it. The clear liquid immediately began to seep out. He didn't need any of the aloe, though, as his hands had become so blistered and hard from the long years of cotton-picking, aloe had no effect anymore. He covertly passed the aloe leaf to the person nearest him, who allowed a few of the drops to fall into the palm of his hand, then passed it on to the next person.

Just then, an entire family came riding by in another rickety wagon being driven by an old grey horse. They were humming an old hymn and praying praises to God.

"Sumpin's going on," one of the young men said under his breath. "We ain't never seen this many niggahs riding horses and wagons. That group of 'em even sound like they's happy bout sumpin. Sumpin's surely goin' on."

"Shut your mouth, boy," one of the elders ordered. "The only thing going on is you need to get back to your work. That's the only thing going on. Don't pay them niggahs no mind. Just get back to yo work," he commanded the boy.

#

"Lunch!" the foreman called out and they all headed for the work wagon where they had left the rations of boiled corn cobs, more pan-fried corn cakes and maple syrup the wives had prepared and placed in tin cans. While eating, they began to whisper amongst themselves.

"What you think goin on, Leroy?" someone asked. "Why all these niggahs coming by heading every which way but south? You think Lincoln done come thru and passed that law freeing all slaves? You think we's free and just don't know it?"

"Stop that blaspheming, fool. You know we ain't free. And if we was, massa sho' wouldn't tell us," Leroy answered. "Lincoln a White man just like the rest of 'em. He ain't got no power to free us. He just one man. Ain't no one man got that kind of power."

"God do," the eldest of the group commanded. "Yes, He's got the power to set us free. God do."

As they returned to their canned meals, someone looked up and saw a shadow in the far distance. He trained his eyes on the shadow and thought it was a wild animal. "What is that?" he asked.

The others looked up and trained their eyes in the direction of the figure which was rapidly nearing them. As it became clearer in view, they realized it was a person running toward them. Whoever it was, they were waving something in their hands, but they could not make out what it was.

"What you think that is, Leroy?" someone asked.

Leroy strained his eyes toward the running figure and answered, "Don't know. Back to workin'."

They all returned to their cotton-picking momentarily, and the figure kept coming. Whoever it was, they were coming fast, and had been joined by more people, all waving something in their hands. Though the workers could not hear them clearly, they could tell the runners were shouting as they rapidly approached. The eldest man in the crowd was the first to stop working. He used his hand to cup his ear and strained to hear what they were saying.

"You'd best get back to work, old man," Leroy warned.

The old man ignored him and took his hat off to shield the sun from his eyes. "Yes, He's got the power to set us free," he chuckled. "He sho' do, and I think He did."

The crowd grew even larger as it got closer, and finally the workers could see who it was and what they were waving. It was their wives and children from the slave barracks waving small, American flags and running as if their lives depended on it. They were all out of breath and could hardly get the words out when they finally reached the field workers.

"We's free!" they all called out in unison. "We's free! Lincoln done set us free!"

They all stopped their work and looked at one another in amazement. It took a full beat before the reality finally set in. Some began to drop to their knees and thank God. Others began to dance in place. Husbands began to hug their wives, and children began to hug one another. One of the women in the group let out a whining soprano voice and sang:

"Yes, He's got power."

As she reached to the Heavens, someone else echoed her, but sounded more like a voice from the mother land and wailed:

"Power."

A third voice chimed with a a baptist run:

"Power."

Finally, one of the stout, short women let out a lion's roar:

"YES, HE'S GOT POWER!"

The original voice finished the sentence as a quiet, sincere, timid statement:

"Yes, He's got power, power to set me free."

The stout, robust lady sang the lead:

"Free from the chains that abound me,

a slave to no man, I'm set free.

Yes, He's got power, power to set me free.

Filled with God's love for all to see,

I've got to tell the world I'm free.

Yes, He's got power, power to set me free."

Everyone joined in and celebrated by singing, dancing, hugging and kissing as they all headed back to the slave barracks to pack their things and get started on the journey to their free lives.

CHAPTER SEVEN

1867. Nashville, Tennessee. The Fisk Free-Colored School had been in operation for just over a
year, and Professor George White had become a very active and valuable employee to the
university. He had organized penmanship classes in one of the sturdy tents, and students were
learning to print and use cursive letters. In the afternoons, he would transform the tent into a
music class where he had begun working with students who showed an interest and some talent
in singing. They were learning to read sheet music and were performing Stephen Foster's songs
such as "Suwannee River" and "Oh, Susana." The Professor was very pleased with their
commitment and their eagerness to learn. Namely, Maggie Porter and Thomas Rutling showed
the most promise, and George White gave special attention and extra time to their talents.

Now 16 years old, Ella Sheppard enrolled into the university in the fall of 1868. Soon after arriving, when Professor White discovered that she played piano he appointed her as his Assistant. Thus, Ella Sheppard became Fisk Free-Colored School's first Colored teacher. In addition to accompanying the students on piano, Ella continued her studies by paying her tuition from funds she earned teaching private piano lessons.

One morning, just as classes ended, a student showed up to the class and informed the Professor that the new school President, Mr. Spence, needed to speak with him and would like to see him in his office forthwith. The Professor saw the last of the students out, tidied up the classroom, gathered up his things and headed to Spence's office. He made his way across the dirt path and past the massive tent that served as the faculty lounge. The aroma of meatloaf and potatoes filled the air and reminded him that he hadn't eaten lunch. He decided he'd stop by and have a meal on his way back to the music room where he was meeting with the small choral group he had managed to assemble.

The door was open when Professor White reached President Spence's office, so he walked in and found Spence standing by the make-shift window of the Administrative Tent, seemingly deep in thought. Professor White announced his presence.

"Good day, Sir. I was told you needed to see me?"

Spence turned his attention away from the window and faced Professor White.

"Yes. Indeed I do, Professor White." He folded his arms and paced back and forth. "As you are aware, the institution is only a year old, and we seem to already be in a bit of financial trouble." He adjusted his wire-rimmed glasses, then looked over the top of the frame, directly at

White before continuing. "This is mainly due to the students not paying their tuitions in a timely manner. Therefore, the institution would like to commission you to act as our Treasurer."

After a moment's silence, and as President Spence waited for his reply, White quizzically responded. "Why, I am honored Sir, I think." George White had never voiced an interest in devoting any additional time to the university, and he had no previous background in finances. However, his dedication to the school and the students brought him great, personal satisfaction. "What all does this position entail?"

"Primarily, you would be responsible for collecting tuition from newly-freed families and for keeping the school's creditors at bay until we can find more funding to keep the school running."

"Well, I don't see any reason why I can't help out in this manner. As you may know, I am very committed and already contribute my savings, as meager as they are, to the university. I'll see if I can come up with some ideas as to how the school can raise funds."

George White turned to leave. As an afterthought, he turned and added. "By the way, I have formed quite an impressive group from the voice classes and I would like the university to grant me permission to take them on a tour of the North. The donations they receive will surely generate some additional income."

Spence let his body fall heavily into the huge, wooden chair behind his desk with a sigh before he answered and his demeanor became less friendly.

"Yes, I've heard something about that and discussed it with the school's new Dean. He thinks it's a bad idea, and so does the A.M.A. Merely a vulgar and risky idea you have come up with for your own self-interest. We will not allow you to exploit the students in this manner. If you come up with a better idea, we'll consider it."

White was taken aback and slightly offended, but he maintained his stature.

"That is an absurd and offensive accusation, Sir. However, I respect the university's position and will come up with some other ideas. Thank you, Sir. I'll be on my way."

President Spence lifted his body from the chair with much effort and exerted another heavy sigh as White turned to leave.

"Very well. Very well. I will leave you to that. Please let me know what you come up with."

"Certainly, Sir. Good day to you."

#

"Good day, Professor White. Missed you in the faculty lounge this morning," Thomas Rutling called out as he finished his work for the day and removed his apron.

"Good day to you, Thomas. How are your studies coming along?"

Professor White removed a wooden tray from the pile and headed for the food line.

"Just fine, Sir. And those penmanship classes are coming in right handy." Thomas hung the apron on a near-by nail, picked up his burlap book bag and threw it over his shoulder. As an after thought, he added, "I was hoping you could help me out with a small problem, Sir."

White set the tray on a table near-by and gave Thomas his undivided attention.

"Sure, Thomas. How can I help you?"

"Well, Sir. There is this girl." Thomas' voice trailed off as he looked to the heavens. "Most beautiful girl I have ever seen."

"Oh, I see," the Professor smiled. "So, what might the problem be, Thomas?"

"Well, Sir. I would like to court her. But I don't know how to approach her. What should I do?"

"That's easy, Thomas. You simply write her a lovely note and feel her out."

"Oh, Sir," Thomas blushed. "I don't think she would take too kindly to my feeling her up."

White could not contain his laughter and let out a loud chuckle.

"*Out*, Thomas. Not *up*. You feel her out. Use the note to compliment her hair style or the way she dresses. Then, you wait to get a response from her. If she never responds, she's not interested."

"Oh, I see," Thomas exclaimed as the light bulb came on in his head. "Feel her out. Thank you, Sir."

Thomas turned to leave and the Professor picked up his tray and entered the aisle to select some foods. As if it suddenly occurred to him, the Professor looked back and called out to him.

"Thomas, maybe you can help me out with a situation."

Thomas stopped and turned to face the Professor. "Why, certainly, Sir. How might I help?"

"The troupe needs a good baritone. Would you happen to know of any students looking to join the group? It would be a great help to me, if you did."

"I can't say that I know anyone right off of the top of my head, Sir. But I'll certainly keep my ear to the ground."

"I've put the word out to some of my colleagues, and I hope to hear from some of them soon. However, if you should know of someone who is already on campus, that would be a great help," Professor White instructed.

"I'll put the word out to some of my friends, Sir. And I'll let you know what I find out."

"Very well. I look forward to seeing you in music class this afternoon," the Professor added as he perused the food behind the counter.

"You most certainly will, Sir. You most certainly will. Enjoy your meal. The meatloaf is exceptionally delicious today."

"I'm quite sure it is, Thomas"

CHAPTER EIGHT

Now in his early 20s, Frederick Loudin relocated to Pittsburgh where he met his future wife,

Harriet Johnson. The two married and moved to Memphis four years after meeting. Music

played a large part in Loudin's life as he taught, learned to play the organ and was a lead singer

in a choir. His experience back in Ravenna, however, had discouraged him from pursuing any

formal education in music.

#

Just a few years ago, back in Ravenna, Loudin's home church was looking for a new baritone to

join the choir. When Loudin arrived for the audition, some of the elders of the church were

seated at a long, wooden table patiently waiting for the next vocalist to appear. The ladies waved

their fancy fans slowly back and forth with a distinguished tilt of their heads in an effort to heed

off the warm weather. The setting sun beamed through the stained glass windows. A handsome

and debonaire Fredrick Loudin straightened his bow tie, adjusted his suspenders and pulled his

already-too-short pants even higher before entering the room with a commanding presence.

Loudin looked past the blank stares, gawks and smirks and gave a polite bow of the head in the panel members' direction. His voice filled the room like a lion's roar.

"Afternoon, Sir, Ma'am. My name is Frederick Loudin. I heard you were looking for a good baritone singer and I would like to audition to sing with your choir."

Loudin extended a black binder containing his resume to one of the members who returned his offer with a blank stare which prompted Loudin to break into song with a pitch-perfect:

"Way back upon the Suwannee river…"

"There will be no more of this nonsense!" one of the panel members yelled.

Another member spoke up in a more calm, serene voice. "We're not sure we are the… right choir for you, Mr?…."

"Loudin. Frederick Loudin."

"Yes. Mr. Loudin. You see…"

Frederick politely interjected. "My family has been members of this congregation for a few years, Sir. My parents raised me as a devout Methodist and I already know you are a fine choir, and…"

"Yes, Sir," someone else cut him off. "We are familiar with your family, however…"

Frederick kindly interjected again as he moved unsteadily on his feet. "And I am quite familiar with your repertoire. Your rendition of *Rock of Ages* is very impressive. However, I thought if you have the baritone hit a D minor at '*let me hide*', he sang, then continued, "it would give the song a bit more… let's say,…"

"No, Sir. You don't seem to understand," another member chimed in. "You see, you people are not allowed to..."

Frederick outright interrupted, this time. "Oh, I beg your pardon Ma'am, Sir. You see, I'm not a slave. I was born of free parents, and..."

"But, you are Colored!" someone exclaimed.

Frederick looked at each member with confusion on his face. He placed his hand over his heart and gave a small bow.

"Yes, Ma'am, Sir. I am Colored. However, I have a very impressive resume. My ancestors are all very fine musicians, and..."

"Coloreds are not allowed to sing in the church choir!" a rude voice trumpeted.

The others at the table nodded in agreement and mumbled under their breaths. The trumpeted voice continued, "Freed slaves, non-slaves, it doesn't matter. Coloreds are not allowed to sing in the church choir!"

"It's just not permitted," one of the sheepish members added as they all rose from the table, pushed their chairs noisily forward and began to leave the room.

Frederick Loudin watched in amazement as they filed out, quietly voicing their opinions to one another. Loudin thought, what good did it do to have been reared in such a fine congregation, doing the work of the Lord, just to be told that he still wasn't good enough to sing praises to Heaven because of his color? He'd heard that slaves had been freed in the north and were beginning to contribute to their churches and communities in various ways. Why was it still different here? Surely, if he could just get a break, he knew he could become a fine choir member, and the Lord would be pleased with his contribution. He should just leave this God-forsaken place, he thought. That's right! That's exactly what he'd do. He would travel north and find a group to sing with who would respect and accept him for his talent. Loudin looked around the beautiful edifice, shook his head from side to side, then began to sing.

"Jesus, my own, to heaven's gone…"

He took in the royal blue carpet in the choir's stand beneath the navy blue, regal thrones that the Pastor and Deacons occupied during Sunday services. Frederick continued to sing.

"I'll never turn back no mo', no mo'."

He looked up at the floor-to-ceiling, stained-glass windows which formed the back-drop of the choir's stand. Loudin slowly turned and began to walk down the aisle toward the door. He looked to the heavens and clasped his hands.

"He whom I feast my hopes upon…"

He lowered his eyes and admired the oak wood floors, which complimented the like-kind oak pews, and he sat in contemplation.

"I'll never turn back no mo', no mo'."

The ornate windows, strategically placed along both sides of the sanctuary, reverberated as he continued.

"No mo', no mo', no mo', my Lord…"

Loudin stood and continued to reluctantly walk toward the massive, hand-carved double doors. He looked back and continued singing.

"I'll never turn back no mo', no mo'."

He raised a fist and shook it in a show of strength.

"His trust I see and I'll pursue, I'll never turn back no mo', no mo',

He reached the huge doors, turned the brass handle, then turned to get one last look at a place he knew he may never see again.

"No mo', no mo', no mo', my Lord. I'll never turn back no mo', no mo'."

#

Now singing with an impressive group in Memphis, Loudin worked on perfecting his craft and rapidly caught the attention of the choir's Director who approached him one evening after a rehearsal.

"Frederick. I would love to speak with you on a personal level; maybe over coffee?"

A beverage made popular after the 1776 Boston Tea Party event, which left some Americans feeling that switching to coffee from tea was a patriotic duty, a cup of coffee sounded glorious.

Loudin readily replied, "Certainly. I would be honored, Sir."

The two men left the room and strode toward the town square. Passer-bys attending to their evening chores busily made their way to their destinations. As they passed the lobby of the town hotel, a burst of laughter from within poured out onto the sidewalk. Simultaneously, a gun shot was suddenly heard in the distance and everyone stopped momentarily, looked into the distance, then continued on their way. The two men shook their heads in shame, but neither commented on the startling event they had just heard.

"I appreciate your contribution to the organization, Mr. Loudin," the Director led in. He tipped his hat toward Loudin, and Loudin returned the gesture.

"Your talent is notwithstanding".

"Why, thank you, Sir. The compliment is greatly appreciated." Loudin adjusted his jacket and stuck his chest out as they entered the saloon, removed their hats and took a seat near the door.

"I must be frank with you, however, Mr. Loudin."

Loudin leaned in.

"Lately, you don't seem fulfilled. It's as though your heart is not into your work."

Loudin cleared his throat, rubbed his chin and nervously shifted in his seat.

The Server approached the table. He met eyes with the Director, shunning Loudin in the process. His voice was a mere whisper as he leaned in to speak to the Director.

"I'm sorry, Sir. This establishment doesn't serve Coloreds. I 'll have to ask this gentleman to leave."

Loudin pushed his chair from the table, but before he could rise from his seat, the Director slipped a $1.00 bill in the Server's hand and placed their order.

"We will have two coffees." He returned his attention to Loudin. "Do you prefer cream and sugar, Mr. Loudin?"

"Yes, Sir. As a matter of fact, I do. Thank you, Sir," Loudin proudly stated as he met eyes with the Server.

"Very well, Sir," the Server reluctantly replied as he pocketed the $1.00 bill and walked away.

Loudin returned his chair toward the table and continued their conversation.

"I'm not sure I know what you mean, Sir."

"Well, I noticed you right away when you first joined the organization. You are an excellent baritone with a thirst for knowledge and technique."

The Server arrived carrying the coffee, cream and sugar. He efficiently arranged the items on the tabletop. The two men added condiments of their choice to the brews, then resumed their conversation.

"That would be an accurate interpretation of where my spirit is right now, Sir," Loudin admitted. He gently placed his spoon on the napkin to his side, then took a sip of his coffee. The Director did the same, then both men nodded in approval of their selection.

"How can I help you with that, Mr. Loudin?"

The Director showed sincere interest in Frederick's plight. Loudin shifted in his seat, once again, as he rubbed his beard and carefully chose his words.

"Please, don't get me wrong, Sir. I thoroughly enjoy being part of the ensemble and take great pleasure in donating my time and talents."

Both men sipped their coffees.

"Go on," the Director encouraged.

Loudin leaned in closer.

"It's just that I know there's more out there for me, Sir."

"Such as? " the Director asked, puzzled.

"Sir, I would love to find a group I can relate to and sing within my own community. The opportunities just aren't there for Coloreds yet. I was even turned down by my own church choir because I am Colored, for Heaven's sake!"

The Director leaned far back in his seat and showed signs of disbelief as Frederick continued. " Coloreds aren't allowed to sing in the church choir. Even if you were born free, as I was."

The Directer relaxed his position, leaned forward and interlocked his fingers.

"I see. I was not aware of that. I've always lived in Pennsylvania, and as you may know, we were the first state to abolish slavery in the United States way back in 1780," he proudly boasted. "I'm still learning the ways of the South; demeaning, though they are."

The men finished their coffees and the Director motioned for the Server to bring more.

"It just came to me, Mr. Loudin. I have an acquaintance who is a fine Director out of Ohio."

Loudin stirred cream into his new cup of coffee.

"Do tell, Sir. Is he a Colored man?"

The Director chuckled. "No, he is not. But, ironically, he leads a Colored ensemble and is very involved in the Colored community."

Loudin rubbed his chin, cleared his throat and leaned in once again.

"Tell me more," he pled.

The Director straightened up in his seat and spoke with authority and pride as his lead was revealed. "His name is Professor George White. He teaches penmanship at the new Fisk Free-Colored school down in Nashville. Actually, because of his wonderful rapport with the Colored students, he is the Treasurer of the university."

"This sounds promising, Sir. However, I have no intentions or interest in attending school. I've already had my fill of the demeaning, outright discrimination in the education system. But, do go on."

The Director finished his second cup of coffee and rose from his seat. Loudin followed his lead as the two men tipped their hats to the Server, then returned them to their heads on the way out of the door. Once out on the sidewalk, the Director continued.

"Mr. White is due in town in a couple of weeks. Here is his contact information."

He found a pen and a strip of paper in his pocket, and a solid surface to write on, then continued as he jotted Professor White's contact information down.

"Why don't you drop him a line and ask for a meeting while he's in town?"

Loudin was filled with hope and could not contain his excitement as he received the note.

"This is wonderful, Sir. I think this is just what I've been looking for," he excitedly exclaimed.

Loudin put the note in his jacket pocket and tapped his pocket for safekeeping.

"I will most certainly pen a note to Professor White this evening, Sir, and will send it the first thing tomorrow. Thank you for such a wonderful lead."

"Not a problem," the Director assured him as he extended his hand to Loudin in anticipation of a hand shake.

Loudin did not disappoint and reached his hand toward the Director, and the two men heartily shook hands.

"There will come a time, Mr. Loudin," the Director predicted, "when *who* you know will be far more important than *what* you know."

"You may be right, Sir. You may very well be right."

The two men chuckled and departed ways.

CHAPTER NINE

Dear Professor George White,

My name is Frederick Loudin and I currently reside in Memphis, Tennessee with my lovely wife, Harriett. I recently enjoyed a cup of coffee with an acquaintance who mentioned your involvement and contributions to Colored students and the arts at the newly-formed Fisk Free-Colored School in nearby Nashville.

As I am a seasoned and trained baritone of utmost talent, I was quite intrigued by the reputation that precedes you in working with accomplished Colored students. My colleague informed me that you would be in the Memphis area in the next few weeks, and I would appreciate a small amount of your time to learn more about this impressive-sounding group of teens. I will prepare a selection to perform for you, and look forward to meeting you while you are in the area. Please respond at your earliest convenience.

Respectfully,

Frederick Loudin

Professor White refolded the letter from Frederick Loudin and returned it to his jacket pocket before he entered the classroom and prepared for the day. As usual, Ella was the first to show up to music class and began preparing the classroom by placing the music stands in orderly rows, erasing the chalkboard, and gathering the sheet music to be used for the day. The university had finally conceded to allowing the Professor to set up singing engagements in near-by towns, and they had been performing all over Tennessee. They gave shows that combined piano, singing, recitations, gymnastics and drama.

As she got organized, Ella found herself humming "Swing Low," Sweet Chariot". Of all the songs she remembered, this song had turned out to be her most favorite of them all. It's lyrics and message always seemed to bring her great peace.

Maggie Porter was the next to arrive to class. As usual, she entered the room with the air of a diva and sat her books on the table with a thud.

"My Lord!" Maggie exclaimed. "I had no idea trying to become a teacher would be this hard. I don't know why I'm putting myself through all of this, when I could just as easily become a performer. It's clear that the Professor takes extra interest in me," she added as she removed her shawl and wrapped it around the back of the rickety, wooden chair.

With her nose in the air, Maggie bragged, "You are aware that Professor White has asked me to take the lead role of *Esther* in Handel's *Cantata of Esther*?" Neither expecting nor waiting for Ella to answer, Maggie continued. "Well, I guess you wouldn't be aware of that, now would you? I was born to play that part," she sighed.

Maggie brushed her skirt before taking her seat, then opened one of her books and began to quietly read. Several other students arrived and took their respective places as Ella continued her work by placing several sheets of music into folders, then placing the folders on the music stands.

"You do have a lovely voice, Maggie. But I'm sure it takes more than a lovely voice to make it in this White world as a performer."

Maggie jumped to her feet, placed her hands on her hips and lashed out.

"Well! Exactly what are you trying to say, Ella?"

Ella knew she had to choose her words wisely, so she let a few seconds pass before answering. She stopped what she was doing and turned to Maggie.

"You have to know how to speak to people, and how to treat people, Maggie."

"I know how to treat people, Ella!"

The other students looked on with interest. They agreed with Ella that Maggie was rude, outspoken and downright mean, and they admired Ella for being honest with her. None of them, surely, had the nerve to confront Maggie themselves. They had witnessed the many tongue lashings she'd given others in the past.

Maggie continued, "I look people straight in the eyes and tell them exactly how I feel. I don't see the need to beat around the bush. In case you forgot, *'we's free'*."

Some of the students nodded their heads in agreement. Others laughed at the exchange. Maggie surely told you exactly what she felt, weather you wanted to hear it or not.

"I know we are free, Maggie," Ella answered with a sly smile. "But *we's* still Colored' .

Just then, Professor White entered the classroom and the students obediently came to order and took their places.

"Good morning to all. I hope you had pleasant evenings. I have a bit of good news and a bit of bad news for you. The bad news is that the school is in dire financial straits and might have to close down."

An outburst overcame the classroom as the students looked at one another in amazement and despair.

Professor White continued. "Quiet down, quiet down, now. As a result, President Spence has asked that I act as the school's new Treasurer. Part of being Treasurer requires that I ask all of you to catch up your tuition fees. I will be visiting some of your parents, attempting to assist them in making this happen."

The Professor moved some papers around on his desk until he found what he was looking for, then he referred to it as he continued.

"Now, for the good news. We've been asked to sing at the Masonic Temple in Nashville. For those who don't know the significance of this, Charles Harrison Mason, an ex-slave himself, has formed a religion he is calling "The Church of God in Christ. The Masonic Temple is where their services are held. It would be an honor to perform here, and we hope to receive a generous collection which can be applied to your tuitions. I'll be holding auditions after classes today for those who would like to try out for a small group which I will take with me. If others of you have ideas as to how we can raise funds to keep the school open, this would be a good time to mention them."

Thomas Rutling raised his hand.

"Yes, Thomas. You have an idea?"

"Yes, Professor. We could follow the route of the underground railroad and sing to our newly-freed families and friends. I just happen to have an unofficial copy of one of the maps. I will bring it to class tomorrow and, maybe, we can plan a short tour of some of the nearby towns."

"That sounds like an excellent idea, Thomas. I look forward to going over that map with you on tomorrow, and we'll see what we can come up with. Now, let's get to work. Let's start with warm-ups."

CHAPTER TEN

Thomas Rutling had mustered up a fine piece of linen paper from Professor White after their discussion regarding Georgia Gordon and 'feeling her out'. Just then, Isaac Dickerson entered the room and sat next to Thomas.

"Good morning, Isaac. How goes your day?" Rutling asked. "I was hoping you had a pen I could borrow."

#

Isaac Dickerson was born enslaved in 1852 in Wytheville, Virginia, and orphaned by the age of five. Union troops overran Wytheville in December of 1864, and though his master escaped on horseback, Isaac was captured. He was marched 75 miles, then eventually paroled. At the time of his parole, he promised to serve as a valet to one of the Union Officers.

One day, Isaac noticed a straggler walking by and realized this man had once been his master's Home Guard. Without giving it a second thought, he ran and ultimately caught up to the straggler. Once he was done explaining who he was, the straggler allowed Isaac to travel along and follow him back to their encampment where he was able to rejoin his master. Two weeks after the close of the Civil War, Isaac Dickerson's master released him. Dickerson ended up in Chattanooga, Tennessee where he worked for a Jewish shopkeeper who taught him to read and write. In 1866, during the Memphis Riot, Dickerson was among the students burned out of a mission school.

#

"What do you need a pen for?" Isaac had asked as he dug around in his satchel, found one, and handed it to Thomas.

Dickerson was now only fourteen years old. However, not only was he a preacher, but he had once taught in Wauhtchie, Tennessee. During that time, he was greeted many mornings by racial slurs and bigoted messages scribbled on the trees throughout the campus. Now, he was a proud student at the Fisk Free-Colored school, attending classes on a racist-free campus and conversing with a fellow classmate in a care-free environment.

"Professor White said if you like a girl, you should feel her out. So, I'm going to write Georgia Gordon a note and feel her out," Thomas told him.

"Feel her out," Dickerson rubbed his chin in contemplation. "What a novel idea, Thomas. Do you think I should do the same?"

"What are you saying?" Thomas asked as he prepared to pen his note to Georgia Gordon.

"I find myself thinking about Minnie Tate all of the time. And believe me, it is not her talent I am thinking about," Isaac whispered, and the two boys laughed.

"Then, you should feel her out, by all means, Isaac. I'll show you my note when I'm done, and you'll get an idea of what to say."

"That would be great, Thomas. And don't forget to return my pen when you're done. Supplies are hard to come by."

Dear Georgia,

My name is Thomas. I wanted to tell you how lovely your hair looked today.

Respectfully,

Thomas

Thomas checked the note for accuracy, then handed it to Isaac who briefly read it and nodded in approval. He retrieved his pen from Thomas and began to write a note of his own.

Dear Minnie,

I like you. Do you like me?

Isaac

#

"What a morning. Good morning, Professor White. What will we be singing today?" Ella asked as she entered the classroom in a mighty rush and found the Professor already there. She was not surprised, however, as she was running late that morning. She had received a letter from the government office that assisted in locating lost loved-ones, notifying her that they had located her real mother. Arrangements were being made to get her mother to Nashville to be cared for by Ella. She had read the letter again and again the night before, and several more times before leaving for school that morning. She spent most of the night fantasizing what it would be like to hear her mother's voice again; to be held in her mother's arms again. She had, long ago, forgiven her mother for almost drowning her as she grew older and saw the perils of mistreatment of her Colored brothers and sisters. Ella came to understand the will to protect yourself and your offspring from the death claws of the White man. Time had gotten away from her, and now she was rushing into class to get things set up before the other students arrived.

"Good morning, Ella. I think we'll start with Stephen Foster's "Suwannee River", then I'd like to begin learning some of the spirituals your ancestors used to sing. With this upcoming performance at the Masonic Temple, I think we should be prepared to entertain the congregation with some of the music they are familiar with. How does that sound?"

"Sounds fine, Sir. I'll get things set up," Ella reluctantly answered.

This was not the first time Professor White had mentioned her teaching her ancestor's music, and she had run out of excuses. The truth was that she was not comfortable with the idea of teaching Colored music to a White man, even though that White man was her teacher. She felt that her ancestor's music was sacred music; meant to be preserved by generations to come. This was music which was usually full of sadness and despair, and told stories of her people's struggles for freedom and of being in bondage. Some of the music even held secret messages in their lyrics, such as "Get on Board…..there's room for plenty more", which may have been a message to others that a group would be leaving via the Underground Railroad that evening, and there was "room for plenty more." *Wade In The Water* is believed to be instruction to wade quietly through the water that evening, for scouts might be out and God was going to *trouble the water.*

Ella wanted to confront the Professor regarding the teaching of the spirituals. However, she was not sure how to approach the subject. Harboring her very conflicting feelings, she decided to just do as she was told and added the lyrics to "Swing Low, Sweet Chariot" to the music folders before placing the folders on the make-shift music stands.

Once all of the students had arrived, Professor White began the class with an announcement.

"Good morning, class. I have quite a pleasant surprise for you today. While in Memphis on business, I recently had the pleasure of meeting a young man who claimed to be a fine baritone, was told about our choir, and wished to audition to sing with us. Though he will not be a student here, and is much older than most of you, I've invited him to become part of our choir, and he should be here today."

As if on cue, a tall, lean, handsome young man who looked to be in his early 20's entered the classroom. He wore a faded, beige suit that looked too short in the pant leg, and a plaid vest that looked too small to button. His shirt was adorned with a bow tie that made him look distinguished. His mustache was thick and bushy, and ended in his beard, which hung impressively below his chin. When he spoke, his voice was like a lion's roar.

"Professor White. It's so good to see you again!"

"And you, Mr. Loudin," the Professor answered as the two shook hands. "I was just telling the students that I was expecting you today. Come. Let me introduce you to everyone."

Professor White took Loudin by the arm and led him around the classroom as he made the introductions. Maggie Porter looked up from the sheet music she was studying and leered at the new-comer in anticipation.

"This is Thomas Rutling, a fine tenor from Wilson County,Tennessee."

"A pleasure to meet you, Mr. Rutling."

"Same here, I'm sure, Sir," Thomas answered with a slight bow of the head.

Thomas kept his eyes on Professor White as he took Mr. Loudin around the classroom and introduced him to the other singers, then slowly pulled the note Georgia Gordon had gently placed on top of his desk earlier from his pocket with great anticipation. His heart had been beating a mile a minute, and his underarms had begun to sweat the moment he placed the note in his pocket. Now, he thought, was a good time to see what she had written.

Dear Thomas,

Thank you for the lovely note.

Georgia

"And this is Maggie Porter, who is about to become one of the Normal Department's first graduates, and aspires to become a teacher," Professor White continued.

"*Miss,* Maggie Porter," Maggie.

"Good to make your acquaintance, Miss Porter. Congratulations on your graduation."

"*Mr.,* Loudin. There's something about you I don't like already, *Mr., Loudin*."

The Professor merely ignored Maggie's comment, as he was used to her abrasive manner. Loudin however, made a mental note of it and vowed to himself to stay clear of her.

"Then we have Georgia Gordon, Jennie Jackson, Isaac Dickerson, an extraordinary baritone and Minister, Benjamin Holmes and Minnie Tate."

Loudin graciously shook all of their hands and moved on.

"And finally, Miss Ella Sheppard, a trained Soprano from Mississippi. She used her talent to raise her $6 tuition, joined us just this fall and has been gracious enough to act as my Assistant. She's doing a fine job, indeed."

Loudin was taken aback by the Professors last comment, and wasn't able to hide his astonishment. "Your Assistant? Why, Professor White. I'm sorry if I assumed, but I thought you asked me to join your group as an accomplished baritone *and* your Assistant. Are you sure a woman is up to this most important position?"

"There it is!" Maggie blurted out. "I knew there was something about you I didn't like the moment I laid eyes on you."

"Simmer down, Maggie," the Professor warned.

"Maggie, there is something about **everybody** you don't like," one of the students added and everyone laughed, except Maggie.

"And your point is?" Maggie snapped, hands on her hips.

"I'm sorry for the misunderstanding, Mr. Loudin, but Ella is doing quite a fine job," Professor White assured him. "Shall we begin rehearsal? Please take your places. Ella, are we ready?"

"Yes, Sir. We are. Mr. Loudin, you can have the spot in the back of the room. You will find the music on the stand. You are capable of reading sheet music, I assume," Ella smarted, but Loudin didn't respond.

#

As she cleaned up after class, Ella found herself still fretting over her mixed feelings regarding assisting the Professor in teaching spirituals to the students. She busied herself putting away the sheet music and the music stands as the Professor busied himself doing his preparations for the next day. Ella's conscious tugged and tugged at her, and in an instant she found herself asking.

"Professor White, may I speak to you, Sir?"

"Why, of course Ella. You seem concerned," the Professor said as he laid the papers aside and turned his attention to her.

Ella circled the row of chairs, which were still arranged in a semi-circle in the middle of the classroom. She clearly appeared nervous and on edge as she spoke.

"Well, Sir, that's because I *am* concerned."

White stood and walked toward her. **"**Please, tell me what is troubling you so."

"With all due respect, Sir, it 'aint right what you doing."

"Isn't. What isn't right, Ella?"

Ella shook her head in shame as she explained. "Having me teach our people's songs like that. Those are sacred songs; songs of our forefathers and the agony of their struggles. It *isn't* right; adding them to our repertoire. It just seems blasphemous, that's all."

Professor White took her by the hand. He spoke softly and sincerely. "I appreciate your concern, Ella, but it is such beautiful music. And that one song, "Swing Low, Sweet Chariot", has become a favorite of mine. It is comforting and assuring. Surely, you can appreciate that."

"Professor White is right, Miss Sheppard," Frederick Loudin, who had been lurking in the wings, interjected.

His unsolicited opinion startled and surprised Ella and the Professor, as neither of them knew he was still in the room.

"Any prudent business **man** can see that we chance bringing in larger crowds when the public hears of our performances of such "**sacred**" music, as you would refer to it," he added.

"I beg your pardon, Mr. Loudin, but this is a private conversation between the Professor and his *Assistant*," Ella snapped at him in disbelief.

"Mr. Loudin is correct, Ella," the Professor agreed, placing his arm about her shoulders. "We must approach this as a business. The institution is slated to close down soon. We must do whatever we can, as soon as we can, to save it. Now, I am holding you responsible for teaching as many spirituals as you can, and incorporating them into our repertoire. Is that clear?"

Ella shot a leering glance toward Loudin, then reluctantly replied, "Yes, Sir. Good night, Sir."

Once she had left the room, Loudin slowly approached with folded arms. "Professor White, I don't know what you see in that young lady's business sense. She is most ineffective as an Assistant, and seems to question your judgement on every hand."

Professor White finished clearing off his desk, rose and ushered Loudin toward the door as he answered, "Miss Sheppard is a very fine assistant, Mr. Loudin".

The two of them walked along the dusty path as they continued their conversation.

"As a matter of fact, " Professor White continued, "when she accepted the position as my Assistant, Miss Sheppard became Fisk's first Colored instructor, and I ask that you respect her as such. And, of course I have asked her to join us for an upcoming tour."

"I'm sorry, Sir? An upcoming tour?" Loudin suddenly stopped walking, as did the Professor. "There is a tour planned? Just my point precisely! Miss Sheppard has made no mention of an upcoming tour."

Professor White resumed strolling along as he explained, and Loudin followed along.

"I asked her not to mention anything to the group until I could, somehow, figure out how to make it happen. It seems our new school President, Mr. Spence agrees with the A.M.A. that touring the group is not a good idea, and they are fighting against the idea on every hand. They have erroneously reasoned that I have a personal interest, rather than the student's and the school's best interest at hand. However, with the university in such financial straits, I've asked Thomas Rutling to bring in a map of the Underground Railroad's alleged route, and I think we will try a small tour to see how things go."

"What do you mean, Sir?" Loudin stopped walking again, which prompted White to do the same.

"The way the students have progressed, it is imperative that the world hear the wonderful music they make. However, since the university does not support my idea of taking them abroad, I thought we might do something closer to home and see if we can encourage the university to sponsor a tour abroad, later in the future. Not to exclude yourself, of course, Mr. Loudin. I hoped you'd consider the offer to travel with us. I think eight or nine singers will make a fine group. I've been trying to contact Maggie Porter, whom I haven't heard from since I cast her as Queen Esther in *Cantata of Esther*." She was a mere eighteen-years-old at the time and studied the part on her own. But, a fine job she did," the Professor fondly reminisced.

"That might be a blessing in disguise, Sir," Loudin chuckled. "I tell you, that woman didn't get along with *anyone*. I've never seen anything like it."

"You may be right, Mr. Loudin," White chuckled. "However, we were so proud to have her become the first Negro teacher to graduate from the Normal Department. The first school she taught at was burned down by the Ku Klux Klan during the Christmas break, but she has persevered and is still teaching at another fine institution. I hear she has moved to Bellevue, some 17 miles away, and I've sent a letter asking her to join us. I hope to hear from her soon."

"If you must, Sir. I agree that some things just have to be embarked upon, Professor White. Please let me know what I can do to assist in making sure it is a successful tour. I would be more than happy to replace Miss Sheppard as your Assistant, if need be."

"Thank you, Mr. Loudin, but Miss Sheppard is doing a fine job."

"And what might you call this traveling, singing ensemble?"

"Why, I haven't given that the first thought. We'll have to get back to you on that, Mr. Loudin. Good day."

"And to you, Sir."

#

Dear Isaac,

I like you, too."

Minnie

CHAPTER ELEVEN

"Professor White, Professor White!" an exhilarated Thomas Rutling shouted as he came running across the dusty lane waving a newspaper in the air. "Have you seen it, have you seen it?" he asked, then skidded to a stop and unfolded the paper so the Professor could see the headlines. "I can't believe my own eyes. Please read it and tell me that it's true."

Professor White accepted the newspaper and scanned it momentarily.

"Yes, indeed, Thomas. I believe you are justifiably excited. It says here, *Thomas Rutling, the best tenor in Tennessee, etcetera, etcetera.* Outstanding, Mr. Rutling. Outstanding, indeed." As he handed the paper back to Rutling, White confirmed, "I thought we might take another look at that map of the Underground Railroad, now that the A.M.A. seems to be softening their position, Thomas. Why don't we go back to the classroom and give it a look?"

The two of them began to walk toward the classroom.

"Surely, you will be accompanying us on our upcoming tour? We'd be honored to have you," the Professor confirmed.

"I beg your pardon, Sir? An upcoming tour? Do you think we might really be able to do a tour?" Rutling could not contain his excitement.

"That's what I said. I've been reluctant to present it to the group because I'm still working on obtaining the institution's blessing. However, if I can muster up enough of you from among the different classes, I'd like to take eight or nine of you on tour. We did such a fine job at the Masonic Temple, we were able to raise $400."

"That's wonderful, Sir. I would be honored," Thomas said as they entered the classroom.

The Professor moved some papers around on his desk, pulled out the aged piece of folded paper and unfolded it atop the desk.

"Let's take a look," he said as the two of them bent over the desk.

The Professor put on his reading glasses and they both studied the states that, allegedly, were part of the underground railroad.

"It looks as though Cincinnati was one of the safe locations, which is a perfect place for us to begin. I have several contacts at Oberlin College. Also, I have plenty of friends and acquaintances in Ohio who will be more than willing to accommodate us."

#

Across from Kentucky, a slave state, Cincinnati was a border town on the Ohio River in a free state. The Ohio River had been used by many fugitive slaves to escape to the north, as far as Canada. Some residents of Cincinnati played a major role in ending slavery by becoming abolitionists, and Cincinnati had numerous stations on the Underground Railroad. Tensions between those who supported slavery and abolitionists caused many violent outbreaks, especially in 1829, 1836 and again in 1842. In 1829, 1,200 Coloreds in the city were attacked in a wave of destruction termed as a 'riot', which caused them to leave Cincinnati and relocate to the north; resettling as far North as Canada. In 1836, a mob of 700 pro-slavery men attacked Colored neighborhoods, as well as a Publisher of the anti-slavery weekly, *The Philanthropist.* Tensions increased even more after congressional passage in 1850 of the Fugitive Slave Act, which allowed for runaway slaves to be recaptured and returned to their rightful owners.

#

"Sounds good to me, Professor. I see Brooklyn was on the route. It looks like the Plymouth Church was a safe haven.

"Yes, I see that. I'll check to see if I have any contacts there. I do remember hearing of a Pastor Beecham who has a very large congregation in that area. Why don't I make some inquiries in those locations and see how things work out?"

"Sounds like a plan to me, Professor. I must be leaving now. Good evening, Sir."

"Good evening to you also, Thomas. And, once again, congratulations on your accolades."

"Thank you, Sir," Thomas called over his shoulder.

"By the way," White added, and Rutling turned around to face him.

"How is your situation with the young lady coming along? Were you able to feel her out?"

Professor White noted the confusion on Rutling's face as he responded.

"Not quite sure, Sir. Not quite sure."

"Maybe you should send her another note, and ask her out."

Rutling sighed in contemplation. "Feeling out, asking out. This liking girls stuff is much more involved than I imagined, Sir. I may take your advice, though, and ask her out. Where should I ask her out to?"

The Professor thought for a moment. "Why don't you ask her out to the upcoming barn-yard dance?" he suggested as the two of them stepped out into the early evening air.

"Excellent idea, Professor White. Excellent idea. Good evening, Sir," Thomas called as he went on his way.

#

Dear Georgia,

It was so nice to see you in class today. I received your note the other day. Thank you for writing me back. I thought you would be interested to know that I have been written up in the local newspaper as "the best tenor in Tennessee". What an honor.

I was wondering if you might be interested in attending the upcoming barn-yard dance with me. Please write me a note and let me know if you would like to come along as my date. Yours, Thomas

#

With a route in mind, Professor White returned to the school's President and asked permission, once again, to take the students on tour. By this time, not only did the school's leaders resist the idea, the A.M.A. refused to give them any financial help, as they had begun holding their own fund-raising events, and didn't want the student's efforts to interfere with theirs. Even White's fellow teachers frowned upon the idea, which made the feat even more difficult.

"We're sorry to disappoint you, Professor White." President Spence raised up out of his chair and walked over to the window. "However, the students still have a lot to learn here at home before we let them go roaming about the countryside. Why, you seem to have no control over these children. How can you depend on the university to trust you to take them out of the area?"

"I'm depending on God, not you," White retorted. "Show some faith in the students and their efforts. Their earnings from the Masonic Temple is proof that they can deliver a performance worthy of revenue. Now, according to my records, there are $40 dollars left in the treasury. I compel you to release those funds and allow the students the opportunity to save their school."

White's passionate plea ultimately swayed the A.M.A., and the funds were released.

#

Dear Minnie,

There is a barn-yard dance next Saturday. Would you like to go?

Isaac

#

"Hi, Georgia. What do you have there?" Minnie Tate asked when she saw Georgia Gordon folding a piece of paper ever so carefully.

Georgia's cheeks blushed as she slipped the note into her text book. "Just a note."

"A note to who? Thomas?"

A look of surprise came over Georgia's face. "How would you know that, Minnie?" she asked in a panic.

"Silly girl. Everybody knows. We see you two slipping notes to one another in class. We're not blind, you know," Minnie smarted.

"Well," Georgia snapped. "We see you and Isaac Dickerson passing notes, too. What do you have to say about that, Minnie?"

Minnie was speechless, as she thought she and Isaac had been careful to conceal their note-passing.

"I say I'll keep your secret, if you'll keep mine."

The girls laughed and agreed. Then, they both pulled all of the notes they had received from the boys out of their books and shared them with one another. Georgia handed Minnie the note she had just finished which read:

Dear Thomas,

I am flattered by your attention, and have asked my parents for permission to allow you to escort me to the barn-yard dance. They have granted me permission. However, please know that my brothers will also be attending as my chaperones.

Georgia

"Did Isaac ask you to the barnyard dance?" Georgia asked when Minnie finished reading, then started writing her note to Isaac.

"Yes, he did, but I haven't answered him yet."

"Well, you'd better hurry up before he asks some other girl," Georgia warned her.

"You're right. I'll do it right now."

Minnie took a pencil and a piece of paper out of her bag and began to write:

Dear Isaac,

Of course, I will go the the barnyard dance with you. What time should I expect you to pick me up? As you know, my brothers will have to escort me.

Minnie

CHAPTER TWELVE

Later that evening n Cincinnati, as promised, Pastor Bennett had arrived and led the children in their bible studies and evening prayer. As they wrapped up, there was a soft knock on the door to the basement. Pastor and Mrs. Bennet looked at one another and nodded, motioned for the students to quiet down, then Pastor Bennett cautiously pulled his gun from his holster and slowly walked up to the door. The children huddled close to one another and held their breaths in fear.

"Who goes there?" Pastor Bennett asked.

The person on the other side mumbled something that caused Pastor Bennett to open the door and allow them in. Once again, the cloaked stranger appeared, handed Pastor Bennett several bags, then quickly closed the door and ran off.

Pastor Bennett re-holstered his weapon, then handed the bags to his wife as everyone sighed in relief.

"Gather around, children," Mrs. Bennett instructed, and directed them to a lone table in the middle of the room.

She reached inside the bags and pulled out cheese sandwiches, as the rations their families had sent had long run out before they ever arrived. Starting with the girls, each student graciously accepted their sandwich, thanked Mrs. Bennett, then moved on. Maggie Porter accepted her sandwich and moved away from the line. Mrs. Bennett watched Maggie from the corner of her eye as she continued to hand out the sandwiches to the boys. Maggie separated the two slices of bread, saw that there was cheese in between them, put them back together, then started to put the sandwich in a trash bin by the table. When she looked at Mrs. Bennett, Mrs. Bennett was looking at her. Maggie rethought her decision, then began to eat the sandwich as Mrs. Bennett nodded her way.

#

Each day, the entire group, along with Professor and Mrs. White and their escorts walked the short block to the venue where the performances took place in the evenings. They rehearsed all afternoon, then received a small snack around 6 p.m. When the curtain rose at 8 p.m. they delivered a stellar performance, Professor White took his bows, then they returned to their hideaway to remain until the next day.

After their evening prayer, some of the students would read, others would write letters back home, and yet others would sit and quietly share their life stories with one another. Ella

Sheppard usually took this time to pen a note to her mother, who had finally shown up in Nashville just before Ella left town for the tour.

Dear Mama,

I'm so glad I found you and I'm sorry I had to leave so soon after getting you back, but I must live up to my responsibility as Professor White's Assistant, and the money I make out here on the road will allow me to continue to take care of you. I miss you already. We have been practicing and working hard every day. I wish I could have brought you with me. It's so beautiful seeing the world pass by from the train. I promise to write to you often, but for now, I must go.

Love,

Ella

The last evening they performed in Cincinnati, the students were met with a warm reception and shown great appreciation at the end of their performance. They took their final bows and headed to the parlor where they usually critiqued their performance amongst themselves.

"We did it!" Ella announced with much pride.

"Yes, I must say, I did give a stellar performance," Maggie boasted.

"Mr. Rutling, you were stupendous!" Loudin complimented.

"As were you, Mr. Loudin," Thomas returned the compliment.

When they entered the parlor, the Professor's wife was sitting at a small desk, counting the night's receipts and rapidly making notes with the aid of a small oil lamp. She'd gone and purchased sandwiches for them earlier that day, and this time they actually contained slices of ham and were nicely arranged on a side table. She had also sought out replacement lodging for them, as some of the town folk had heard about the children lodging in the basement and threatened the property owner. Mrs. White turned around to face the group as the students entered the room with much excitement and glee. The Professor followed close on their heels with great apprehension concerning their receipts for the evening. He surmised by his wife's wide smile that they had done quite well.

"Well, how did we do?" he discreetly asked as he kissed her lightly on the cheek.

"Fifty dollars! What a wonderful night! The university will be so pleased," she whispered to him.

"The university!" the Professor scoffed as he stood over her and looked at her notes. "The university that voted against our touring, and donated a mere $1 toward the effort? Is that the university you're referring to?"

Mrs. White stood and assisted the Professor with removing his tuxedo jacket as he loosened his bow tie. He then let his body plop down in a seat next to her. Everyone poured themselves cups of hot tea; compliments of Pastor Bennett's wife, as they had been taught by the Professor that the warmth would preserve their vocal cords. Ella prepared and delivered cups of tea to the Professor and his wife, then returned to her peers. The students wrapped their necks with warm scarves and huddled close together by the fire to stay warm, as not one of them had an overcoat or a wrap. They chatted quietly amongst themselves as they patiently waited to hear how well they had done that evening. Frederick Loudin found a used newspaper on a side table, held it up to a lantern and began to read.

"If not for the student's desire to save their beloved Fisk, I would have already disassociated myself with the university," the Professor quietly assured his wife.

"Now, now dear," Mrs. White consoled. "It is an honorable feat you and the students have embarked upon. Don't spoil it with feelings of regret."

"And to think I promised them at least $20,000 before we return," he sighed as he rubbed his forehead. "Well, let's inform the students of how well they did and get some rest before we depart tomorrow. Where is our next stop?"

"Columbus. However dear, I hate to inform you that I was not able to secure lodging for the students this evening. My contacts all fell through. Whatever will we do?"

"Don't worry. I'll think of something. God always prepares a way."

"I'll finish up here while you speak with the students," Mrs. White said, and returned to her note taking.

"Oh, my God!" Loudin suddenly shouted, and an eery silence fell over the room as everyone turned their attention toward him.

"Is there a problem, Mr. Loudin?" the Professor asked.

Loudin opened the paper wider and began to read aloud.

"There's a great fire in Chicago that has burned for 2 full days and has killed up to 300 people!"

Gasps filled the room as the students moved closer to get more details.

"Which part of Chicago? I hope it's not on the south side. I have many kin there," one of the singers feared.

Loudin read on. "The fire started somewhere in an alley behind 137 DeKoven Street."

"Oh, my God," the student shouted. "That's on the south side. Professor, I must send a wire immediately. My grandparents live very near there."

Ella Sheppard closed in and and put her arm around the student's shoulders to console her.

"And I have 2 aunts and several cousins near there," another student announced.

"Fret not, children. I'll have my wife send a wire first thing tomorrow. She will use the emergency information you have on record to contact your families," the Professor assured them.

"Read on, Mr. Loudin. What else do they know? How did the fire start?"

Loudin continued to read as the students waited with abating breath. "One theory is that a Mrs. O'Leary was milking her cow when the cow knocked over an oil lamp and started a fire in the barn." He turned the page. "Another theory being looked into is that the fire started when a gentleman known as Daniel "Pegleg" Sullivan ignited the fire while trying to steal milk."

"Some people will stoop to anything to stay alive," Maggie said as she shook her head.

"However," Loudin continued. "The Chicago Tribune has reported the cause to be a group of men led by Louis M. Cohn who has admitted he was gambling in the O'Leary's barn with the O'Leary's son and some other neighborhood boys. When Mrs. O'Leary came out and ran them off, someone knocked over an oil lamp in their haste to flee."

"Heathens," Maggie retorted and shivered as she returned to her seat. " I bet they didn't leave the money behind, though. However it happened, Mrs. O'Leary has got herself a problem."

Loudin moved closer to the light, adjusted the position of the paper and read on.

"Because nearly all homes, the sidewalks and many of the city's roads are made of wood, it aided the fire in spreading faster. At least 100,000 residents have been displaced. What a tragedy."

"Go on. What else does it say? Is it out yet?" the Professor inquired.

"Initially, the firemen were sent to the wrong location, and an alarm sent from an area near the fire failed to sound off at the courthouse where the fire watchmen were, making the rescue efforts take even longer."

"That wouldn't have happened, had it been a White neighborhood," Maggie claimed.

"They hoped the Chicago River would slow the fire down, but the numerous lumberyards, warehouses, coal yards, and bridges fed the fire, and it made it's way to the central business district! Oh, my God. How could this have ever happened? This is a complete travesty," Loudin exclaimed.

He turned the page again, stood and paced as he continued to read.

"After it jumped the river, a burning timber lodged on the roof of the city's water works, the building was destroyed and there was no water left to fight the fire. So it continued to burn, unchecked. This is devastating. I wish there was something we could do to help."

"Yes, Professor. We must do something to help our people. Let's detour and make a performance in Chicago, at once," someone suggested.

The other students voiced their opinions in a moment of confusion and despair until Pastor Bennett interceded.

"Before we make such an important decision, we must take a moment and pray."

They all held hands, bowed their heads and the Pastor sent up a fervent prayer.

"Dear most gracious, heavenly father. Father of Abraham, Isaac and Jacob. Most holy and precious Lord. We come to you with bowed down heads and heavy hearts to ask a special blessing upon our friends and loved ones in Illinois. Our hearts are sad and burdened by the pain we know they are going through. We trust you to lift their bowed down heads. We trust you to uplift their burdened hearts. We trust you to protect them as they flee from their homes, and cities, seeking safety. The children are feeling discouraged and unsure about their destiny. We ask that you strengthen their confidence and uplift their spirits. Give them the courage to know that they can persevere until the end to uphold their commitment to the university. We love you, Lord. We honor you and we lift you up. We thank you for sacrificing yourself on the cross for our sins. We pray that you give us the courage and strength to press forward, and not turn back. In the name of the precious Son of God, Jesus. We say amen, and amen."

When he was done they all said "amen", and a calm came over the room.

Professor White returned to his seat. His wife stood obediently by his side as the students slowly gathered around them and anxiously awaited their decision.

"We were fortunate enough to earn $50 tonight, which was very good, though it's a long way from the $20,000 we've promised the University. Doubling back to Chicago is not an option. However, how do you feel about sending the proceeds from tonight's performance to the city of Chicago? Shall we take a vote on it?" the Professor asked.

Everyone raised their hand, except Maggie Porter. She threw her nose up in the air and turned her head away.

"Very well. I will have my wife wire the funds to the Mayor of Chillicothe tomorrow. Now, let's get some rest. We leave for Columbus early in the morning."

Remembering what his wife told him earlier regarding the lodging situation for the evening, or lack thereof, the Professor amended his statement by making a suggestion. "Actually, why don't we just make our way over to the train station now? That way, we're sure to be on time for the early train.

#

Dear Mama,

We heard about the great fire in Chicago. We were all so sad and we sent the proceeds from last night's concert to the victims. It was not much, but like you always say, every little bit helps. We are leaving for Columbus early tomorrow, so we're staying at the train station tonight. I think we are really staying at the train station because no one will let us lodge in their inns. It's not quite like I thought it would be out here, mama, and I can't wait to get home.

Ella

#

The students were the first aboard the train very early the next morning after they had used the station's bathroom facilities and prepared themselves for the day's journey.

"Next stop, Columbus! All aboard!" the conductor shouted.

As the train chugged along, Isaac took this time to pen a note to Minnie, whom he hadn't spent any time with since the barnyard dance before they left Nashville. It turns out that some of Minnie's relatives had been affected by the great Chicago fires, and were left homeless.

Dear Minnie,

I'm sorry you are sad about your relatives back in Chicago, but always remember that God builds a fence of protection around us as we walk through the valley in the shadow of death. Please have faith that your family is doing well. I will be praying for you.

Isaac

When they reached Columbus, Ohio, Mrs. White made contact with the host families they were depending on to house the children. Unfortunately, the families had been threatened by some of the locals when word got out that they would be hosting Colored kids in their homes. Making the situation worse, the group lacked funds because they had donated the proceeds from the previous performance to the city of Chicago. Therefore, the Professor suggested they remain at the train station while he, Pastor Bennett and some of the male singers went looking for lodging. The students got as comfortable as they could on the old, oak benches, and used their nap sacks for pillows. Some of them actually dozed off. Just as well, as the Professor and the others were unable to find alternative lodging for the evening.

This situation very much discouraged the students, and Maggie Porter was not shy about expressing her feelings about it. Laying adjacent to Ella, Maggie complained in a hushed voice.

"We had fifty dollars, sent every penny to Chicago, and now we have nothing for ourselves. This is disgusting and discouraging," she complained. "I think we should return home to Fisk at once."

"We can't turn back now, Maggie," Ella whispered. "Things will get better. You just watch and see. As we have been taught to have faith, things will get better."

Having trouble getting comfortable on the hard benches, some of the other students who also weren't asleep, quietly agreed with Maggie and began to complain. Yet, others were simply happy to be away from home. Pastor Bennett caught wind of their discouragement and instructed the students to get out of bed and go down on bending knees. He then began to pray.

"*Oh, merciful and ever-loving Father, we come to you with bowed down heads, heavy hearts and defeated spirits, believing that you are the almighty and everlasting God. We believe you have already paved the way for us, and right now, the students need to be encouraged. We trust you to intercede on our behalf and pave the way for us to continue on this most challenging, yet important journey. We beseech you to remove all doubt, fear and anxiety. Assure them, Father, that they are on their destiny's path that you have ordained for them, and that they must persevere if they want to see all of the blessings you have in store for them. We thank you for keeping us thus far, and we go forward believing you will keep us till the end. We humbly submit this prayer in the name of your precious son, Jesus, and claim the victory right now. We trust that you have heard our prayer, and it has already been answered. Amen and Amen.*"

All of the students agreed by saying "amen." Then they returned to their benches and all of them dozed off.

#

The troupe eventually found success in Oberlin, Ohio at a performance that took place before a national convention of influential ministers. After singing the few standard ballads, they began to sing spirituals. Namely, "*Steal Away*" and other songs associated with slavery. This was one of the first public performances of this type of music, as it had only been sung behind closed doors and in the fields.

They ended the show with a rendition of "*Swing Low, Sweet Chariot*," and the audience sprung to their feet and gave them a full three-minute standing ovation. They were so enthralled by the student's performance, this engagement paved the way for their future success as word spread about the wonderful Colored singers from Nashville, Tennessee.

CHAPTER THIRTEEN

The train's wheels screeched and screamed as the conductor brought it to a slow stop.

"This stop is Connecticut! Everybody off the train! Connecticut!" he announced.

Another stop on the Underground Railroad, Connecticut played a major role in supplying the Union forces with weapons and supplies during the Civil War. The state, as small as it was, furnished 55,000 men to the Civil War formed into thirty full regiments of infantry, including two in the U.S. Colored troops. Several Connecticut men became generals, and James Ward of Hartford was the first U.S. Naval Officer killed in the Civil War.

#

Once again, the students arrived at the station where a clandestine figure showed up and briefly transacted business with Professor White. As usual, Frederick Loudin lurked in the wings. Everyone was escorted to a near-by building where they were suspiciously secreted. This stop, they had arrived at Beacon Falls, Connecticut, just north of Seymour, a town that had just been incorporated that same year. It was a 9.8 square-mile Indian camping ground, and artifacts such as arrowheads had been found on the land. They repeated the same ritual as they had done in previous cities; snuck in, placed their belongings under their cots, had their evening bible study and prayer, dined on cheese sandwiches, then retired for the evening.

After several evenings of performances, they were hurried to the train station and boarded.

By this time, some of the students began to experience terrible coughs, tuberculosis, strep throat and various illnesses. Their worn clothing began to shred into rags, but they pressed on.

"Next stop, Rhode Island. All aboard!"

#

In 1774, the slave population of Rhode Island was 6.3%, nearly twice as high as in any other New England colony. However, during the American Civil War, Rhode Island was the first Union state to send troops in response to President Lincoln's request for help. Rhode Island furnished 25,236 fighting men, of whom 1,685 died. On the home front, Rhode Island and the other northern states used their industrial capacity to supply the Union Army with the materials needed to win the war. When slavery ended in 1866, Rhode Island abolished racial segregation in public schools throughout the state.

#

The group had arrived at Newport, Rhode Island, home to Captain Simeon's Potter House where Professor White had secured actual rooms for the students. Unlike their previous stops, they were welcomed through the front door of the inn, but were ushered up the rear stairs, as the Innkeepers didn't want to take the chance of insulting any of their White patrons who paid a hefty price for the luxurious accommodations offered there. The students were taken to the maid's quarters where they were given real beds, though they had to sleep 2 to a bed. They were supplied with exquisite products from New York-based *Kiehl's*, which included their original Musk Oil and Blue Astringent Herbal Lotion. They were also provided with house robes, and slippers. The evening meals included day-old bread with butter and honey, warm tea and fresh fruit. Lunch was usually luke-warm soups and stale sour-dough breads, and dinner was usually corn cobs and chicken legs. Things were looking up, and they began to feel encouraged. Not even Maggie Porter complained on this stop, notwithstanding that she wanted to.

The students continued to perform night after night, and though they received warm receptions, the collection plate barely made up for their expenses. Because of lack of funds, they eventually returned to sleeping at the train station in the evenings, even though the Professor, Pastor Bennett and some of the male students continued to wade through sleet and snow, seeking lodging for them. However, more often than not, no lodging was made available.

When it was discovered by the town-folk that they were lodging at the train station, they were mistreated by the press and labeled as "vagrants", "poor panhandlers" and "underprivileged Coloreds". Having read this in the papers, their audiences began to show a lack of interest and appreciation during their latter performances. Some attendees conversed loudly amongst themselves as the students sang, and others simply walked out during the performance. The students ate, had religious studies, prayed, slept, then arose the next morning, just to do it all over again. One morning, they were treated with warm tea and tea cakes for breakfast, then ushered off to rehearsal. Once again, they rehearsed all day and sang late into the evening. At this point, they had been on the road an entire year.

Dear Mama,

These people are so mean. They are calling us vagrants and panhandlers. We sing so beautifully, and they hardly put anything in the collection plates. I'm doing my best to stay encouraged, but itCs getting harder and harder to do. I can't wait to get back home.
Ella

When this leg of the tour finally ended, they were elated to head for the station early one morning where they boarded the train when they heard the conductor call out, "Next stop, Massachusetts. All aboard."

#

Pre the American Civil War, Massachusetts was a center for the abolitionist, temperance and transcendentalist movements. One of the students' performances at this stop was at the World's Peace Jubilee and International Music Festival in Boston, Massachusetts. Architect William G. Preston had designed a 100,000-seat arena at the cost of $500,000, specifically for this event. Acts came from as far as London, Berlin, Germany, Paris and Ireland. One concert featured a performance of Verdi's *Il Trovatore,* performed by a 2,000-member orchestra, 100 assistants and a 20,000-voice chorus. The Fisk Jubilee Singers' performance at this event marked the first time African-American singers were included in a big musical production in the United States.

One evening, Professor White stole away from the group and meditated in a personal prayer of his own, asking God for direction. It troubled him that the group was being billed merely as 'Colored students from Fisk University, Nashville, Tennessee'. They needed a name. White picked up his bible and was led to the 25th chapter of the book of Leviticus where he read about the year of Jubilee. Each fiftieth Pentecost was followed by a "year of jubilee" in which all slaves would be set free. He reasoned, since the students were newly-freed slaves, of course they should be called the "Jubilee Singers". White rubbed his long, narrow beard and smiled with satisfaction. He would inform the students first thing in the morning.

The next morning, after all of the students had gathered in the assigned location, Professor White proudly made his announcement. "You shall be called the Fisk Jubilee Singers, in reference to the year of jubilee in the bible."

Maggie Porter put her hand on her hip and leaned back. "You would think we would be called '*Maggie Porter and the Fisk Singers*', since I'm the one most often showcased."

"And the one most often forgetting her lyrics,"someone retorted.

"Well, I never," Maggie snapped.

Professor White ignored their spat and continued.

"Very well, then. The Fisk Jubilee Singers, it is."

Dear Mama,

The Professor has decided to call us the Fisk Jubilee Singers. Maybe we will get more respect, now that we have a name. We are on our way to Baltimore, then Washington, D.C. where we are actually going to sing for the President of the United States! How exciting is that?

Ella

After a few days on the train, the conductor finally called their station. "Next stop, Baltimore."

#

In 1861, Federal units and state regiments were attacked as they marched through Baltimore. This caused the Baltimore war of 1861, the first blood shed in the Civil War. However, the bloodiest single day of the Civil War, the Battle of Antietam, claimed nearly 23,000 casualties and was fought in this area. This battle was considered a Union victory and a turning point in the war. By 1810, before the war, the free Black population increased from less than 1% to 14% in this area. Revolutionary ideals, influences of the changing economy and preachings of ministers resulted in numerous planters in Maryland to free their slaves in the 20 years after the Revolutionary war. Maryland remained with the Union during the Civil War, and by 1860, 49% of Maryland's African-Americans were free Blacks.

#

The group arrived near Baltimore Inner Harbor at a building that later became the Admiral Fell Inn. It was a basic, four-story, cubed, brick building with beautiful french windows. To their surprise, the students were allowed to enter through the front door, they were allowed to take the front stairs up to their rooms, and they were allowed to actually sleep in the beds.

Pastor and Mrs. Bennett assisted the children in settling in. The girls ran around the room touching and feeling the fine artifacts, bronze statues and crystal candy dishes filled with candies. They were even allowed to have a piece of the candy. They smelled the flowers, looked out of the windows and decided which of the many teas they would have later. Minnie and Georgia had never left the powder room since they had arrived. They smelled all of the soaps and lotions, played with the fixtures and looked in the mirror, a lot.

"This is really nice," Georgia whispered.

"I can't believe we're here. I wonder what Maggie Porter has to say about this." Minnie said, and the two girls laughed. They both looked in the mirror and mimicked Maggie Porter by placing their hands on their hips and leaning back. Then they said in unison, "My name is Miss, Maggie Porter." The two of them bursted into laughter, once again.

"Shh!" they warned one another as they put their fingers up to their lips.

"Did you see that fancy restaurant on the way in?" Georgia asked.

"Yes. Wouldn't it be nice to be invited to dinner in that fancy place tonight?" Minnie day dreamed.

"And sit next to Thomas and Isaac and hold hands?" Georgia whispered, a gesture Minnie would never have brought herself to think of, otherwise, and caused her to blush.

Both girls jumped up and down and shrieked with glee, like the school girls they were.

"Shhh!," Georgia warned.

"Well, we know that will never happen. Not with the Bennett's watchful eyes.

"No, that will never happen," Georgia sadly agreed.

At the same time, Frederick Loudin had ventured downstairs and was touring the inn. A bald-headed Black man came rushing out of the kitchen in a mighty hurry wearing a tall, white hat, a white, food-stained apron and wielding a meat cleaver. He startled when he laid eyes on Frederick.

"What you doing here, boy?" he quipped, clearly interrupting his stride and coming to a skidding halt.

"My name is Frederick, Sir. Frederick Loudin." Loudin tipped his hat and gave a short bow. The man raised a brow. "I'm with the Fisk Jubilee Singers, a choral ensemble from Nashville. We come on behalf of the Fisk Free-Colored School, and we specialize in harmonious melodies, some of which are actually Spirituals. It's lovely to be here in your fine city, Sir."

"Look here, boy," the man shook the cleaver as he spoke. "First of all, you ain't got to call me 'Sir', okay? "Next," he continued, "You shouldn't be walking around here by yourself. Now, I heard you say something about 'students', 'singing'; you know I heard the word, *Colored*, and I think you mentioned the town of *Nashville* somewhere in there. All that other stuff you just said don't mean nothing to me. Follow me," he suddenly ordered, pointing the meat cleaver toward Loudin.

Frederick followed in faith, attempting to keep up with the man's rapid gait.

"So, tell me some more about you and this singing. Who you singing to?" he asked as they walked down a long hall past several rooms.

"For Fisk University, si…." Frederick caught himself.

"Leroy. Just call me Leroy," the man said.

"Leroy," Frederick gave him a polite bow.

"You sho' is formal, boy. Where was you a slave at?"

"I have never been a slave, Leroy."

"That so?" he asked.

When they got to the end of the hall, Frederick looked to his right and noticed a lovely dining room with white linen table cloths, fine china and crystal flatware and stemware. The room was aglow with a golden aura emitting from the candles in the wall sconces. Fresh flowers adorned each corner of the room, and the lilies gave off a pleasant fragrance.

"So, you was born free?"

"Yes, Leroy. I was born free."

Loudin suddenly stopped and wandered into the room. Once he realized Loudin was no longer beside him, Leroy stopped and looked back. He watched Frederick enter the room as if in a trance.

"There are nine of us," he told Leroy, though he was clearly being distracted by all of the beautiful surroundings. "We are traveling with our choir director, Professor George White and his wife." He picked up a fork sitting at one of the place settings and pondered over it's intricate detail, then gently placed it back on the table. "And Pastor Henry Bennett, the school's Preacher, and his wife," he continued.

Loudin slowly walked around to the other side of the table as the man looked at him in disbelief. "We've come a long way in a short time, and we press on, in faith," he said as he rejoined the man at the door, and they continued on their way.

"We are on an 18-month tour, and we sing to Coloreds and Whites along the route of the Underground Railroad."

"You don't say?"

"Yes. It's a fund-raising tour on behalf of the university, Leroy. The school is in financial straits and we are attempting to raise funds to keep it open."

"You mean people pay money to hear ya'll sing?"

"Yes, they do."

Leroy finally stopped in front of two huge, steel doors, faced him, and motioned the meat cleaver in Loudin's direction.

"You hungry, boy?" he asked as he grabbed a heavy jacket from a hook on the wall and motioned for Loudin to do the same. Then he put on a heavy pair of rubber gloves and offered

Loudin a pair. Leroy opened one of the huge doors with a hefty tug, and a mist of cold air escaped from within.

"Well, yes, Sir," Loudin admitted. "I could use something to eat."

Both men shivvered.

"However," Loudin continued, "I am traveling with 12 other people, and it wouldn't be polite to dine without including them."

"I tell you what. Let's make a deal. You go in there and get me some supplies, and I'll take care of you and your friend's meals in that lovely room you were so interested in."

"Really, Sir? I would be honored. As I mentioned, though, there are 13 of us."

"I heard ya," Leroy cut him off, then motioned for Loudin to enter the freezer. "Old man can't deal with that cold air no mo'. Fields got the best of my days. I'm just trying to hold on, boy. I'm just trying to hold on."

Leroy retrieved a rolling cart from the corner and pushed it up to the door, then stood as far away from the door as he could, shivered and bundled himself up in the jacket while he gave Loudin directions.

"I need some of them steaks over there on the right, top shelf."

#

Ever in the powder room, Minnie and Georgia took turns fixing one another's hair. One of them found what Mrs. Bennett had taught them was a comb and brush and they began to practice putting one another's hair into different braided styles.

"So, have you let Isaac kiss you, yet? Georgia pried.

"Oh, my God, no, Georgia. I would never do such a thing. Well, until I get married, anyway," Minnie emphatically stated. "Would you?" she asked.

"I don't know. I might. Isaac is so handsome, I just might."

The girls quietly giggle. Minnie had some fancy ribbons, so she tied one to the end of Georgia's braid. "It really would be nice to sit down and dine like the White folks," she envisioned, looking up at the ceiling.

"Yes, it would. Maybe we should pray for it," Georgia suggested. "Pastor Bennett always says if you want something, don't steal it, pray for it. So, let's pray for it."

The two girls looked at one another and agreed just as Mrs. Bennett walked up and heard Minnie begin to pray.

"Dear Father in Heaven, the Father of Abraham, Isaac and Jacob, we come this afternoon to thank you for this wonderful trip and this wonderful room. We have been taught to trust you for all of our needs, so we want to let you know that we need to be invited to dinner in the restaurant of this fine hotel tonight."

"And allowed to sit next to Isaac and Thomas. And hold hands. Amen", Georgia added.

Mrs. Bennett smiled and moved away from the door.

#

"One box of them steaks outta do," Leroy called into the freezer to Loudin. He stepped back as Loudin appeared at the door carrying a cold, heavy box and dropped it on the cart. Leroy positioned the box where he wanted it to be, then continued. "I need a couple of them prime ribs hanging from those hooks up there, and one of them hogs."

Loudin went in, reached up and unhooked one of the prime ribs, brought it out and sat it on the cart, then went in and retrieved the other prime rib and hog.

"Some potatoes, on the other side, bottom shelf," Leroy continued.

Loudin found the potatoes and broke into a sweat as he lifted the heavy, fifty-pound bag and placed it on the cart.

" I need some of them eggs, too; I need a bunch of 'em." Leroy rubbed his chin in contemplation, then continued, "Let's say two crates of them eggs. Right side, above the potatoes."

Frederick found the eggs and carefully placed them on the cart.

"And some of that butter. One of those tubs outta do. Right in the middle of the shelf. "

Frederick rolled the heavy tub out and Leroy assisted him in placing it on the cart, closed the door and the two men removed their coats, returned them to the hooks and started their trek back to the kitchen, Frederick insisting on pushing the cart. On their way back, Leroy confirmed their agreement.

"So, I can expect thirteen people for dinner, say, 7 o'clock in the Victorian Dining Room, correct?"

"What a lovely gesture, Sir. I'm sure the group would be very grateful for your kindness."

"There you go with that 'Sir' stuff, again. I guess that's just your way."

Just then, they made it back to the kitchen. "So, I'll see you and your guests at 7 o'clock, Frederick."

"Thank you, Sir. However, I wouldn't want you to jeopardize your position here to accommodate us, Leroy."

"Always remember, boy," Leroy added. "It's who you know, not always what you know. And you just happen to know the head chef. What I say, go, around here. See ya'll at 7."

"You most certainly will, Sir. You most certainly will."

#

"Georgia, Minnie, would you girls like to let the other girls have a chance in the powder room?" Mrs. Bennett called to them.

Both girls looked at one another, then into the mirror one last time, laughed, then ran out of the powder room as a knock was heard on the door. When Mrs. Bennett opened the door, it was Pastor Bennett. He bent momentarily as she greeted him with a kiss on the cheek, then the Pastor became serious, turned to the girls and made the announcement.

"Good evening, young ladies. You are to be commended for the fine jobs you are doing on behalf of the university. Please know that the university, wholeheartedly, appreciates your contributions. With that said, we have made arrangements for you to enjoy a wonderful meal from the restaurant. They will bring you your meals at 6 p.m. That will be all."

Pastor Bennett turned to leave, and when he opened the door, Frederick Loudin was rushing by, noticed Pastor Bennett and stopped.

"Pastor Bennet, I was just coming to see you."

"What might I help you with, Frederick?"

The door was still open, so Mrs. Bennett and the girls listened to the men's exchange, as Loudin seemed elated, and they wanted to know what was going on.

"We have just been invited to a private dining room by the inn's chef, Sir. They are expecting us at 7 p.m. in what they call the Victorian Room."

That was all the girls needed to hear. Minnie and Georgia looked at one another in shock.

"It works!" Minnie shouted. Prayer really works!"

"It most certainly, does, Minnie," Mrs. Bennett agreed.

Bennett raised his eyebrows. "How did this come about, Frederick?"

"It's a long story, Sir. But I would love to tell it to you over dinner."

"Very well. Until 7 p.m. Wonderful news, Frederick. Wonderful news."

#

Wearing the best attire they owned, the entire group showed up in the lobby at 7 p.m., sharp. Leroy came out of the kitchen and met them.

"Frederick, he said," as he approached.

"Hello, Leroy. These are my guests. Professor and Mrs. White," he pointed.

The Whites bowed his way and Leroy returned the gesture.

"Pastor and Mrs. Bennett," he continued.

More bows took place.

"This is Ella Sheppard, Minnie Tate, Georgia Gordon, Mabel Lewis, Thomas Rutling, Isaac Dickerson, Benjamin Holmes, Daniel Cole and Miss, Maggie Porter."

Everyone bowed and expressed their appreciation, then Professor White spoke on behalf of the group. "This is a wonderful gesture on your part, Sir, and we most appreciate it."

"Not a problem, Sir," Leroy caught himself saying. "Any friends of Frederick's are friends of mine. Now, ya'll follow me this way. I'll get you seated, then my staff will come in and attend to you."

They all raised their eyes at one another, then followed Leroy down the long hallway to the lovely "Victorian Room". Minnie and Georgia held hands as they walked along and viewed the wonderful art on the walls. When they entered the room, a harpist began to softly strum the strings, and beautiful music began to fill the room.

"Professor White and Pastor Bennett, why don't the two of you take these head seats at each end of the table, and your wives can sit to your right. Then we can put the girls on this side and the boys on this side," Leroy suggested.

Mrs. Bennett thought about the prayer she heard Minnie and Georgia send up earlier, so she made a suggestion.

"Thank you, Leroy, but I thought we would do something a bit different this evening," she said, addressing the students. "As you are all maturing and will have to learn to interface sooner or later, why don't we sit boy, girl tonight?"

Leroy raised an eyebrow toward Loudin, who returned the gesture.

" Minnie, why don't you sit next to Isaac, and Georgia, you take the seat next to Thomas. Ella, I would love to sit near you, and Miss, Maggie Porter, why don't you sit next to Daniel Cole. Is that okay with you girls?"

Minnie and Georgia's eyes widened as they smiled at Mrs. Bennett who winked an eye at them and smiled. Pastor Bennett looked at his wife over his glasses as he and Professor White pulled back the chairs for their wives. Isaac, Daniel and Thomas took note and pulled the chairs out and allowed the girls to take their seats. Once everyone was seated, and before the food ever arrived, Minnie and Isaac were holding hands under the table, as were Thomas and Georgia.

Suddenly, Colored butlers and maids arrived and placed several baskets of freshly-baked breads and butter pats in several positions on the table. The students admired the fine china and silver pieces. They studied the many bronze candlesticks with tall, flickering candles adorning them. Soft music continued to be played in the background as the harpist suddenly began to strum the melody to the opening song from *"Cantata of Esther"*, and Maggie Porter could not restrain herself. She stood and sang along with the music, then everyone, including the staff applauded her wonderful rendition. Maggie took her bows and as she returned to her seat, Daniel Cole took her hand in his and squeezed it. Maggie blushed, then pulled her hand away. Pastor Bennett led a prayer.

Precious, Heavenly Father. Thank you for this meal, thank you for those who are assisting us along our way, and thank you for our continued health and strength. May this meal be received with humble hearts, and may it be enjoyed by all. Amen.

The children began to pass each bowl around the table, helping themselves to the prime rib, fresh fish, boiled corn, mashed potatoes, and green beans.

#

"Well, this isn't so bad," Maggie admitted after that wonderful meal, and as they changed into their night clothes that evening.

"I'm glad you finally approve," Ella said.

"I didn't say I approve. I merely said that it's not so bad."

"Maggie, Maggie," Ella sighed as she shook her head from side to side.

CHAPTER FOURTEEN

Ulysses S. Grant, a West Point graduate, once served in the Mexican-American War.

He retired from the Army in 1854, but civilian life was not kind to him. Therefore, in 1861 when

the Civil War broke out, Grant re-enlisted into the United States Army where he rapidly rose

through the ranks. After his victories in the Chattanooga Campaign, in March 1864 President

Abraham Lincoln promoted Grant to a Lieutenant General, then ultimately to a prominent United

States Army Commanding General. As such, Grant worked closely with President Lincoln to

lead the Union Army in overcoming the Confederates. Grant had bloody battles on several

occasions with Robert E. Lee during the Civil War, and Lee finally surrendered to Grant at

Appomattox, VA which fundamentally ended this legendary war in 1865. Slavery officially ended in 1866.

After Lincoln's assassination, the country's new President, President Andrew Johnson appointed Grant to a position implementing Reconstruction. However, Grant and Johnson often bumped heads, prompting Grant to run for and, eventually, get elected as President, himself. During this time, although they had not been granted the right to vote, many Blacks considered themselves Republicans. Grant led the Republicans in an effort to remove the very shadow of Confederate nationalism and slavery.

Grant served two terms as President of the United States; some criticizing his Presidency as being lackluster. This was primarily due to his failure to alleviate the economic depression following the Panic of 1873. Grant's monetary actions during this critical time caused interest rates to rise and made matters worse for those in debt. During a time when businesses were expanding, money became scarcer to obtain. This action caused 18,000 businesses to fail between 1873 and 1875.

Believed to have been caused by American post-Civil War inflation, rampant speculative investments, the loss of the value of silver, a large trade deficit, property losses in the Chicago and Boston fires, and other factors, the panic was ultimately known as the "Great Depression." The massive strain on bank reserves plummeted in New York City during September and October 1873 from $50 million to $17 million. The crisis lasted from 1873 until 1879, and beyond for some countries.

Others, however, regarded Grant as a President who took strong action on civil rights for African-Americans as early as the early1870s. His goal was to protect African-American citizenship and to support economic prosperity.

When Professor White received communication from the White House asking that he bring the singers to perform for Grant's inauguration, the Professor proudly accepted on behalf of the students. In addition, a separate performance was scheduled for Vice President Schuyler Colfax and members of the U.S. Congress.

After the performance, the students looked forward to staying overnight in one of D.C.s fine hotels. They stood by and anxiously awaited direction from the Pastor's wife. They all had visions of grandeur as they boarded the wagons and headed for the hotel district. The wagon pulled up to the Georgetown Inn, and 'oohs' and 'aahs' were heard throughout the wagon.

"I don't know why you all are getting so excited," doubting Maggie Porter told them. "These White folks are not going to allow us to stay in their fine hotel. You mark my word."

"Oh, Maggie. Why do you always have to be so doubtful and negative?" Ella asked. "Why can't you just keep hope alive and trust God to intercede on our behalf? All White folks are not bad White folks."

Maggie adjusted her hat, then her shawl and stuck her nose up in the air. "No, they are not, Ella. However, good or bad, they are not going to allow us to stay in their fine hotel." With that, Maggie turned her head away and scooted over in the seat, not wanting to be near the others.

As the Pastor and his wife led the children to the lobby and positioned them out of the way of the other guests, Professor White and his wife approached the front desk to check in and obtain keys. The students spent their time quietly conversing and discussing all of the wonderful

artifacts and floral arrangements in the lobby. Maggie stood alone and away from the others

with a pessimistic look on her face as she watched White people go to and fro.

"Move, gal," a rude White man snapped as he passed by her and continued on his way.

"My name is Maggie. Miss, Maggie Porter. Not, gal," she said, even though the man

had long gone about his business.

After a while, the Professor and his wife approached with keys to their rooms.

The students carried their own bags and headed for the back staircase where they made their way

up the three flights of stairs. The Bellman carried Professor and Mrs. White's bags, along with

Pastor Bennett and his wife's bags, and led the four of them to the elevator. Once upstairs,

Pastor Bennett and his wife used the keys to get the students into their rooms and settled.

Mrs. White had efficiently obtained a two-room suite for the girls and Mrs. Bennett, and

another one for the boys and Pastor Bennett. The children explored the rooms with excitement

and glee, as the rooms were equipped with all of the latest amenities available. The beds were

soft and dressed with wonderful linen, beautiful drapes adorned the oak bay windows, and there

were floral arrangements and beautiful baskets of fruit on the dresser and table. The girls began

to unpack their bags and put their personal items into the dresser drawers. All except Maggie.

She merely sat in a corner, holding her bag, and waited. A small desk was in one corner with

fine stationery and fancy writing implements on it.

"My mama would love this stationery," Ella commented, and she sat down and began to

pen a note.

Dear Mama

We have been gone for almost two years and I am ready to come home. I am sick of dealing with pompous Frederick Loudin, and that rude Maggie Porter is embarrassing and always looking to pick a fight. We get to come home for two weeks, but we must leave again to finish up the tour on the eastern part of the United States. I look forward to seeing you soon.

Ella

#

"Let's go see the powder room," one of the girls suggested with glee. "I bet it is most beautiful, and has a toilet!"

"See there, Maggie? And you thought they would not let us stay here. This place is beautiful," Georgia Gordon commented.

"The night is not over, yet, Georgia. Before the night is over, we will probably be asked to leave," Maggie predicted.

The other girls ignored Maggie, giggled and ran off to find the powder room. There was suddenly a knock at the door, and Mrs. Bennett opened it to find herself face-to-face with a hotel employee. "Good evening. May I help you?" she asked with a smile.

The visitor appeared uneasy and nervous. He barely made eye contact with Mrs. Bennett as he attempted to look past her, into the room, as he spoke. "Good evening, ma'am. I am sorry to trouble you, but the Bellman informed me that there are Colored kids occupying this room?"

"There are," Mrs. Bennett proudly announced. "They are the students from Nashville that sang for President Grant yesterday, and Vice President Colfax today. Would you like to meet them?" she asked.

"I'm sorry, ma'am, but the students will have to leave."

"Excuse me?"

Maggie Porter stood up and started for the door. The other girls returned from exploring the powder room as Mrs. Bennett turned to face them. They could immediately tell that something was troubling her, and their smiling faces went away and were replaced by looks of disappointment.

"Girls, please get Pastor Bennett," she instructed.

The girls all ran to the connecting door of the suite and knocked rapidly.

"This is unjust and un-Christ-like of you to ask the students to leave. May God have mercy on you," Mrs. Bennett chastised.

When Pastor Bennett opened the door, he did not have to ask the girls what was going on, as he saw his wife standing at the door to their suite with the door open. He entered the room and walked up to greet the visitor by extending his hand as he approached.

"Good evening, Sir. I am Pastor Henry Bennett, clergy for the Fisk Free-Colored School. How might I help you this evening?"

"Good evening, Pastor." The visitor shook Pastor Bennett's hand, then continued. "As I was informing your wife, you and your wife are welcome here, but I am afraid that your students will need to depart from the hotel."

"Why, whatever for?" the Pastor asked, clearly upset.

"I am sorry, Sir. They should have told you at the desk when you checked in. Coloreds are not allowed to lodge here, Sir."

"Do you know who these students are, young man?" Bennett demanded with a voice of authority. "These students just performed at President Grant's inauguration yesterday. I demand to see the manager at once!"

Maggie Porter walked past the man and turned her nose up. "Hmmph," she uttered as she passed, then went and waited in the hall for the others, who had started to remove their items from the drawers and return them to their make-shift pieces of luggage.

"I am the manager, Sir. I am sorry about the confusion, but we had no idea that Professor White was securing rooms for Coloreds. You can stay, but your students will have to leave. I am sorry."

"What you should be is ashamed, young man. Not sorry. Very well. We do not want any trouble. We will depart at once."

"Henry!" Mrs. Bennett exclaimed as the Pastor closed the door behind the visitor. "Is that all you have to say about this? How can you let them treat these children this way?"

"Just get the young ladies together and meet me in the hall, dear. I will notify Professor White and gather up the young men," Pastor Bennett instructed his wife.

All of the girls were dutifully standing alongside Mrs. Bennett, awaiting instruction, with sad faces. She ushered them all out into the hallway where they waited for Pastor Bennett to gather up the boys, some whom had already gone to bed for the evening, and were fast asleep.

"I knew it was too good to be true," Maggie announced. "We will never get the respect we deserve in this unjust country. White folks will never change."

"Oh, shut up, Maggie!" Minnie and Georgia sang in unison.

#

When they all had gathered in the lobby, Professor White approached the desk. Frederick Loudin stood in the wings to witness the exchange about to take place. He always took every opportunity to learn from the White folks how to transact business, and this, indeed, was an opportunity. The manager approached and extended a hand to George White.

"Professor White. I am sorry for this misunderstanding, Sir."

The two gentlemen shook hands. "There is no misunderstanding, young man," George White asserted. "We are in your fair city as guests of the President of the United States of America. These students are the elite, celebrated Fisk Jubilee Singers from the Fisk Free-Colored School in Nashville, Tennessee. We have paid your asking price for our rooms, and we are already settled in. What is the meaning of your asking us to leave?"

"As I have already stated, we are sorry for the misunderstanding, Professor White. We had no idea you were paying for lodging for Coloreds. Coloreds are not allowed in this hotel. You and your guests are welcome to stay, but the others must leave immediately."

"This is ludicrous!" Loudin voiced.

White motioned for Loudin to calm down. "These students *are* my guest, Sir. However, if you will not allow them to lodge here, you can return our funds and we will be on our way."

"Very well, Sir," the manager said and went to retrieve the Professor's funds.

Loudin took a step back and collected himself. Then he turned and walked toward the other men of the troupe. As he approached them, Thomas Rutling stepped away from the group and pulled Loudin to the side.

"What's going on?"

"They're kicking us out of the hotel. Coloreds are not allowed to lodge here," Loudin informed him.

"Well, let's do what we do," Thomas Rutling sighed. "I think I saw a hotel at the corner. Let's go see if we can stay there."

The two men exited the grand lobby and spilled out onto the sidewalk. Once outside, they both looked up the street in one direction and down the street in the other. Horse-drawn carriages slowly passed by and stirred up dust from the road. Couples strolled along, holding hands and cheerfully laughing.

"There," Loudin pointed. "Let's see if we are welcome at this place."

The two men headed off toward the direction of a hotel on the next block.

Only one block away from what was then called "President's Square," the boys found a grand hotel that was a clear 2 blocks long. The sign in the window said, 'Wormley House'. The building was three stories tall and had six large, white pillars on each side of the impressive oak doors. A grand balcony sat atop each set of pillars. At the front entrance, an awning was arranged forming a covered way from the street to the front door. Several regal-looking horse-drawn carriages were parked out front. The trees out front were adorned with small, flickering lights.

Once inside, the sound of lively music and brilliant lights flooded the lobby. The two young men were awe-struck at what they found. They looked in one direction and saw several Colored maids waiting to take care of the guest's wraps. Finely-dressed Colored people were mulling about freely, seemingly without a care in the world. The men wore fancy top hats and the women wore furry mink stoles. The aroma of fine cigars filled the air. Coloreds were sitting confidently in restaurants, sipping on cocktails, and waiting to be served without prejudice. The front counter was actually staffed with people who looked just like them; Colored. They wore like-kind uniforms of starched white shirts and calf-length burlap skirts. Their hair was styled in fancy up-do's, and adorned by flashy hair ornaments. The two Colored Bellmen stood at attention, waiting to be needed.

On the opposite side, four broad parlors were put together to form a magnificent salon. On the main wall was a gold-framed copy of a very official-looking document, so the two of them slowly walked up to it and began to read. It contained the wording of the 13th amendment, and had what looked like over 150 of the original signatures on it. They looked at one another, then back at the document several times before proceeding.

#

Having arrived in the 'President's Square' area of Washington, D.C. around 1815, Lynch Wormley, a Black man, had once engaged the services of Francis Scott Key, a prominent lawyer at that time, to assist him with a law suit against Smith Cocke for Wormley's certificate of freedom. Lynch wished to conduct business in the D.C. area, and such a document was required to do so. Francis Scott Key wrote the "Star Spangled Banner," which was later adopted as the national anthem.

James Wormley, one of Lynch's sons was actually born in President's Square adjacent to the west side of the park. He had started his business career as a jockey at the race tracks around Washington. After a successful lawsuit, Lynch and his sons, who were experienced horsemen, developed a successful livery business as hack drivers. They serviced politicians, socialites and businessmen.

Once his father started up the hack business, James went to work for him, and was privy to private discussions of very prominent men of that time. Because he had shown that he could maintain confidentiality regarding the many private conversations he overheard, he became a favorite of these men.

James learned the trade of being a professional host by catering to the needs of the elite after he became a steward on steamships. Later, he became steward at the Washington Club, a very impressive private club during that time. The club catered to the likes of Jefferson Davis, William Corcoran and George Riggs. Wormley built and maintained relationships with some of these most powerful people. In the early 1850's, James had purchased houses on I Street between 15th and 16th Streets, N.W., and had developed his own restaurant and hotel business utilizing these houses.

The Washington Club closed in 1859, and the members would hold their meetings at Wormley's restaurant on I Street to discuss the future of the defunct business. In 1860, the first Japanese Commission was sent to Washington, and Wormley was engaged to cater a sailing trip they took up the coast from Norfolk to Washington and on to Philadelphia. His services were so highly regarded that in 1867 Secretary of State William H. Seward commissioned him to have the next Japanese Commission accommodated at Wormley's houses on I Street. He ultimately developed these properties into Wormley House, the only Black-owned hotel of that time. Wormley House became a favorite among the nation's top military and political leaders during that era. Also, musicians and literary figures, alike, frequented the hotel. The inn offered all of the amenities of a fine, White hotel, including a barbershop, bar, cafe and restaurants, and catered mostly to the upper class of political White men in the city and their guests. However, Frederick

Douglas, John Mercer Langston, who was the first Dean of Howard University Law School and Thomas Edison were also known to frequent the establishment. Wormley, himself was known to be a personal nurse to the likes of Henry Clay, Daniel Webster and Abraham Lincoln, just to name a few.

#

Dazed, Rutling asked Frederick, "Is this for real?"

Loudin straightened his jacket and brushed his mustache and beard, to assure that his appearance was impeccable, before the two men cautiously walked up to the counter. They were acknowledged immediately by a pleasant, smiling middle-aged Colored woman.

"How may I help you gentlemen this evening? Wait a minute," she added suddenly as her eyes widened. "Aren't you two of the students from Nashville who sang for the President yesterday?"

People standing nearby heard her, took notice and started to mill around with curiosity. Loudin stuck his chest out, grabbed his lapels and boastfully rocked back and forth on his heels.

"Yes, we are. My name is Frederick Loudin and this is Thomas Rutling, the best tenor in Tennessee. Thank you for acknowledging our accomplishment, ma'am."

The people standing nearby started to whisper and spread the word, and before long, a crowd had gathered around the young men.

"What an outstanding job you students did. We were so proud to see you at the White House. And your singing was absolutely divine."

"Thank you, ma'am," both men replied.

"What ever can I do for you young men this evening?"

"It seems as though we have been asked to leave the Georgetown hotel up the street; because we are Colored. I trust that you can accommodate us here."

"Absolutely, Mr. Loudin. Will it be just the two of you?"

"No, ma'am," Rutling assured her. "The rest of the group is still at the Georgetown. Shall we retrieve them and let them know that we can be accommodated here?"

"You most certainly can. How many rooms will you be needing?"

"We usually require two suites for the females, two suites for the males and a room for Professor White and his wife," Loudin explained.

"Oh, that won't nearly be enough. Why don't we put two people per room and set you all up with several rooms? You go retrieve everyone, and I will get your room keys ready. We would be honored to have you as our guests. I'm sure Mr. Wormley will be honored to take care of all of your expenses during your stay here."

"Why, thank you, ma'am," the two young men said as they bowed and turned to leave.

"It's them," they heard someone in the crowd to say. "It's really them. It would be lovely to hear them sing something."

Frederick and Thomas rushed back to the Georgetown to get the others, who had already loaded their belongings on the wagon and were ready to leave. Their faces were filled with disappointment and sadness. An excited Rutling could hardly wait to get there and give them the good news.

"Professor White, Professor White, you won't believe it! There's a Colored hotel up the street. I mean, there's a hotel up the street that allows Coloreds! And Colored people work at the hotel, Colored people are milling around the hotel, and I see Coloreds actually dining in the restaurant!"

The other students overheard Thomas' rendering of the news and were overcome with excitement. They moved over to make room for him in the wagon so that he could tell them more. Even Maggie Porter seemed to lend an ear, as this sounded promising. Frederick Loudin stood outside of the wagon and filled Professor White and Pastor Bennett in on their findings.

"Can they accommodate us?" Professor White inquired.

"They most certainly can, Sir," Loudin assured them. As a matter of fact, the kind lady insisted on giving us several rooms, at no charge, Sir. I must warn you, though. She actually recognized us, and word rapidly spread as to our identity. The guests are very excited about our coming there, and are hoping to hear us render a selection. I think it would be an excellent idea to accommodate them, Sir. I hope you agree."

"That sounds wonderful, Mr. Loudin. Excellent job on your behalf."

"Thank you, Sir. Shall we be on our way?"

"Absolutely."

By the time the group arrived, unloaded their bags and headed toward the lobby of Wormley House, a large crowd had formed inside.

"Here they come!" someone shouted and everyone began to applaud as they entered. Maggie Porter checked her appearance, straightened her hat and lifted her head. She pushed her way to the front and strutted like the diva she was. To the onlooker's surprise, the group formed a semi-circle, Professor White retrieved his baton, the piano in the background stopped and a hush fell over the entire lobby.

Someone whispered, " They're going to sing! This is absolutely wonderful!"

Professor White's baton slowly began to move and the children began to sing. They performed "In Bright Mansions", a'capella.

In bright mansions above,

In bright mansions above,

Lord, I want to live up yonder,

In bright mansions above.

My mother's gone to glory,

I want to go there too,

Lord, I want to live up yonder, up yonder,

In mansions above

My sister's gone to glory

I want to go there too

Lord, I want to live up yonder

In bright mansions above.

My brother's gone to glory

I want to go there too

Lord, I want to live up yonder

In bright mansions above.

My Savior's gone to glory

I want to go there too

Lord, I want to live up yonder

In bright mansions above.

A chant of The Lord's Prayer was recited at the end of the song, as the women held a soprano note for what seemed an eternity. As they sang, every now and then they noticed flashes of light from what they assumed were newspaper men taking photos. They also noticed passer-bys coming into the lobby to witness their performance. When they were done, there was a long pause, then the crowd suddenly burst into an overwhelming applause. They clapped, whistled, and yelled 'bravo'. Some on-lookers were seen wiping tears from their eyes. The students took their bows, as did Professor White, then someone in the crowd approached and presented Pastor Bennett with a hat that someone had passed around, now filled with money, for the students.

The students stayed in formation as some of the spectators approached and congratulated them. Others asked for their autographs. A news reporter approached with his pad and pen in hand, and Maggie Porter took a step forward.

"Good day, kind Sir. My name is Miss, Maggie Porter."

The reporter jotted down, *Maggie.*

"Miss, Maggie Porter," she repeated, then waited and watched while the reporter amended his note, *Miss, Maggie Porter.*

"And where are you from, Miss, Maggie Porter?" he asked, and prepared to write down her answer.

"I am from Lebanon, Tennessee, a first-generation free-slave." Maggie looked down at his pad as he made a note of that. "I have been a member of the Fisk Jubilee Singers since it's inception in 1868 and I am the stellar lead Soprano."

Maggie made note of his note, then continued. "In 1870 I sang the lead role in Handel's *Cantata of Esther* under the direction of Professor George White. I was the first Colored to graduate from the Fisk Free Colored School's Normal Department, and I have taught at many schools myself. Would you like to know anything else?" she asked.

"No, thank you. I'm sure that I can get a story out of the information you gave me. Thank you for your time, Maggie."

"Miss, Maggie Porter," she corrected him as he walked away.

A man holding a huge, bulky camera approached the group. "Children, may I get a picture, please?" he called out.

Everyone returned to their concert positions and proudly posed, some standing around the piano and some sitting on the piano bench. He set his camera up, stood behind it and pulled what looked like a black veil over his head. All of a sudden the students were momentarily blinded by a bright flash of light.

The students had never had this type of attention and closeness with their audience before, and they found it exciting and exhilarating. When they finally made their way to their suites, using the elevator, they all went to bed feeling victorious, as they had finally been recognized and celebrated for their hard work.

#

Dear Mama,

We got kicked out of the hotel in Washington, D.C., even though the President of the United States had invited us to sing for him. We were all sad until we found another hotel that was owned by a Colored man! It was as fancy as the hotels the White people have. Everyone there was glad to see us, and we sang a song right there in the lobby. The newspaper people did what they call an interview with Maggie Porter, and they took a real, professional picture of us.

They even took up a collection for us, and the Professor allowed us to divide the money equally

and put it in our pockets! I'm going to buy you something real nice, mama, and bring it home

with me.

Ella

#

"Next stop, New York City!" the conductor called out as he passed through the cars.

While in New York, the troupe spent six weeks performing at Steinway Hall. This is also when the males of the group recorded "Swing Low, Sweet Chariot; the first music ever recorded by African-Americans. In December the singers arrived in Brooklyn to perform at Henry Ward Beecher's weekly prayer meeting at Brooklyn's Plymouth Church. Henry Ward Beecher was an abolitionist and the brother of Harriet Beecher Stowe, who wrote "Uncle Tom's Cabin". He was also the son of one of the best-known evangelists of his age, Lyman Beecher. Leading up to the Civil War, Henry raised money to purchase slaves from captivity and to send rifles (nicknamed "*Beecher's Bibles*) to abolitionists fighting in Nebraska and Kansas. He became the pastor of the church in 1847 and was known for his novel style of preaching which included humor, dialect and slang, and thus acquired him fame.

Not only did Beecher allow the students to perform at his church, he made accommodations available to them during their stay. The student's performances were so widely celebrated, every church wanted the Jubilee Singers from that point on. Their appearances began to attract national attention and generous donations. Audiences began to warm up to their style, as they were not performing minstrel-like music in blackface, which is what White musicians normally did to entertain audiences. By now, they had become largely responsible for the popularization of the Negro Spiritual style of singing as a form of entertainment. The tune of some of the newspaper articles began to change, and they were now being written up as singers who were doing "great work for humanity." Beecher was so moved by the student's talents, he commanded his wealthy parishioners to give freely to the Jubilee Singer's cause.

However, the students were met with mixed opinions about their performances by the local newspapers. The *New York World* called them "trained monkeys" who sang with a "wild darky air." The *Newark Evening Courier* listed them as if they were items from a slave-sale catalogue. They mentioned nothing of their talents; only of their physical characteristics.

#

Dear Mama

We have been gone for almost two years and I am ready to come home. I am sick of dealing with pompous Frederick Loudin, and that rude Maggie Porter is embarrassing and always looking to pick a fight. One of these days, she's going to end up getting thrown off of the train. We were glad to leave New York. I hope to never return there. Everybody moved around too fast. It seemed as though we had to rush everywhere we went.

We're coming home for two weeks, but we must leave again to finish up the tour on the eastern part of the United States. I look forward to seeing you soon.

Ella

#

"Did you see all of those White folks?" Ella whispered to Maggie as they wrapped their necks in warm scarves one evening after a concert.

"Yes, I did. However, White folks do not impress me the least bit."

"Oh, Maggie. You are always so negative. Do you get pleasure from anything, at all?"

"Yes. I plan on getting pleasure out of that comfortable bed they have for us at the hotel. It's been so long since my head has hit a soft pillow, I may not want to get up early tomorrow to return home."

"Oh, I'm sure you'll be able to force yourself up and out of here. We've been away from home absolutely too long."

#

With less than two week's rest, the singers were back on the road touring the Eastern United States. This finalized their debut tour, which lasted 18 months, and by the time they returned to Nashville in the spring of 1873, Professor White and the students delivered the full $20,000 White had promised.

CHAPTER FIFTEEN

On their first day back to school, the students were all glad to see one another as they rehashed

all of the wonderful adventures they experienced to the other students who hadn't joined them on

the trip. Professor White entered the classroom and took his place at the podium as the students

mingled about. Thomas removed the note from Georgia from his pocket and read it.

Dear Thomas,

I wanted to thank you for being such a gentleman while we were on tour. I am honored that such a fine gentleman as yourself would notice me. I had a wonderful time at the dance, and hope we can do it again. My brothers think you are very kind and respectful.

Until we speak again,

Georgia

"Quiet down, class. Quiet down. Welcome home. You are to be commended for your performances and stamina as we traveled about these United States. It was an exhausting, yet lucrative tour, and your efforts are much appreciated. Shall we begin rehearsal? I love the impromptu medley we performed at the station in 1871 before we left, and thought we might work on putting another group of Spirituals together for our future performances. Let's look at *Every Time I Feel The Spirit.*"

As he raised his baton to gain the student's attention, Dean Cravath entered the classroom.

"Professor White. So good to see you all back again. May I have just a moment with you before you begin your class?"

"Of course, Sir."

"I just stopped by to say how grateful the school is for your group's contributions. We can hold our creditors off a while longer because of their efforts, and we have cleared the land to begin construction of the first permanent structure on the campus. There's talks of naming it *Jubilee Hall.*"

The students noisily congratulated one another. All except Maggie Porter and Fredrick Loudin. They both rolled their eyes around in their heads and stayed quiet.

"On that note, I'm pleased to inform you that the university has received communication from abroad, and the group is being asked to travel to Britain to sing for the Prime Minister, Sir William Gladstone."

Everyone's eyes widened, and sounds of pride and glee filled the room as the students contemplated such a wonderful opportunity, though they had no idea who Prime Minister William Gladstone was or where Britain was. Dean Cravath let them take in the good news for a moment, then continued.

"That's not all. Queen Victoria, herself, has asked that we perform for her while in Britain."

Everyone gasped with excitement, including Frederick Loudin. Everyone except Maggie Porter. She jumped to her feet.

"Queen Victoria! What would Queen Victoria know about the Fisk Jubilee Singers? Where is this Britain, anyway? Will we get paid for our performances?" she shot questions off like bullets.

"I trust you can have the group ready by April," Dean Cravath added, totally ignoring Maggie's ranting.

"April!" Frederick Loudin stepped forward and shouted. "Surely you're aware that we've just returned from a very long, eighteen month, exhausting tour, Sir. In light of the fact that we have yet to be compensated, in any manner for our efforts, I'm sure I speak for the entire group when I say that we need time to rest our voices and prepare ourselves for such a prestigious endeavor."

"And we need to be compensated for our time already invested," Thomas Rutling added.

"Maybe your age has an effect on your health, Mr. Loudin, but I assure you the rest of us are fully capable of being prepared by April," Ella commented, and the other students laughed.

"You tell him, Ella," Maggie chimed in. "But, I agree with Thomas. When will we be paid for our time and talents?"

"I tend to agree with Mr. Loudin on this point Sir," the Professor commented. "The singers are, indeed, exhausted. However, we'll put it to a vote and get back to you, if that's acceptable."

With that said, Professor White raised his baton in preparation of beginning rehearsal.

"I'm sorry Professor White, but you seem to think this is a request. There will be no voting. Please have the students prepared to embark in April. They will be sailing over on the beautiful Holland America cruise ship. What an honor. What an honor, indeed," Dean Cravath stated as he turned and left the room.

"I vote 'no'," Maggie shouted. "Cruise ship or no cruise ship. I'm tired of having to sneak into dirty hotels and sleeping on train station benches. I don't have to live like that. I can always return to the theater where I was respected and treated like a professional singer. My back hurts, my feet hurt and Professor, sometimes that food the Bennetts muster up just...Lord have Mercy. I don't even know what to say about that, except that it's hardly fit for human consumption."

"Come now, Maggie. You heard the Dean. I trust you will be prepared to leave in April. Now, let's begin rehearsal."

#

After school let out, Dean Cravath returned to Professor White's classroom as White was in the process of preparing to leave for the day. White walked around the room and blew the flames out in one of the sconces as Cravath entered.

"Professor White, may I speak with you?"

Startled, Professor White turned around to face him, then blew out another candle.

"Of course, Sir."

"It has been called to my attention that two of your singers are in danger of being expelled from the school."

White was surprised by this news, and it clearly showed in his expression as he spoke.

"Really? I was not aware of that. Whatever for, may I ask?"

White blew the last candle out, and a darkness fell upon the room except for the lantern he picked up off of his desk to assist them as they departed. The two men began their walk across the campus.

"Professor," the Dean continued in a hesitant voice, "as you are aware, this is a Christian school with Christian rules and regulations. That is why we hold prayer and read scriptures from the Bible each morning before classes commence. It is important that the newly-freed teens develop moral compasses, in addition to their regular studies."

"I'm not sure I know what you mean, Sir. Whatever blasphemous thing are these two young men doing?"

The Dean appeared embarrassed as he spoke. "Thomas Rutling and Isaac Dickerson have been passing notes to two of the female students in your class. As a matter of fact, please send them to the administrative tent in the morning after prayer and scriptures. We are considering expelling them from the school for their un-Christ-like behavior."

The Professor recalled his conversation with Thomas before they left on tour, and sheepishly turned his head away and smiled.

"I'm sure that this situation can be rectified, Sir. I will speak to both of them at once, and reemphasize the university's position. With the next tour coming up so soon, I wouldn't be able to replace them in time, as their talents are exceptional and not easily replaceable. I'm sure you understand, Sir."

"Send them to my office first thing in the morning," Cravath demanded, then went his own way.

#

On their way to Dean Cravath's office, Thomas and Isaac contemplated their dilemma.

"What do you think this is about?" Thomas asked.

"I can't imagine. Maybe they want to ask that I start leading the morning prayer. I am a clergy, after all."

"I don't know, Isaac. I don't think this is a social call, if they called both of us in. I have a very uneasy feeling about this."

Just then, Georgia and Minnie called out to the boys from the other side of campus.

"Hello Thomas and Isaac," they sang in unison as their cheeks blushed. The girls continued on their way, giggling the entire time.

"Hey, girls," the boys called back.

When they reached the Dean's office, Thomas knocked lightly on the door. Isaac stood behind him and sheepishly peeked over Thomas' shoulder. They heard the Dean call out to them.

"Come in, come in."

The two boys entered the room and dutifully approached the huge desk where the Dean was perched. He removed his eyeglasses and laid them on the desk, then directed the boys' attention to two wooden chairs.

"Have a seat, young men."

Thomas and Isaac did as instructed. Once they were seated, Cravath merely stared at them during an eerie silence. Isaac shifted uncomfortably in his seat and Thomas felt beads of sweat develop on his forehead. Cravath stood and walked toward the window as he spoke with his back to the boys.

"It has been called to my attention that you two boys have been writing notes to some of your female classmates."

Both boys felt lumps develop in their throats, but neither knew what to say, so they both stared at one another, but remained silent. Their chairs squeaked ferociously as they shifted uncomfortably in their seats.

"As you know," the Dean continued, "fraternizing with the opposite sex is forbidden by the school's by-laws. Therefore, it is my belief that the two of you should be suspended from the university."

Both boys' hearts began to beat rapidly, and the beads of sweat that had formed on Rutling's forehead now began to run down his face, but he dared to wipe them away.

"Sir," Rutling started in.

The Dean cut him off. "However, because of your relationship with Professor White and the upcoming tour, the Professor has informed me that your contributions to the choir are irreplaceable, and he has assured me that he will be keeping an eye on you fellows from this point on. There will be no more note-passing between the female students. Is that clear?" He finally turned and faced the boys.

"Absolutely clear, Sir," Rutling managed to voice.

"Mr Dickerson?"

"Yes, Sir. That is absolutely clear, Sir."

"Very well," the Dean said as he returned to his chair and let his body fall down into the leather cushion.

The boys remained in their seats, afraid to move a muscle.

"That will be all. You are excused. Please close the door behind you."

The two boys immediately rose and hastily departed as they wiped the sweat from their brows.

CHAPTER SIXTEEN

Later that spring of 1873, George White, Pastor Bennett, their wives and the singers

arrived to the boarding dock to embark for their second tour abroad. By then, the students had

upgraded their wardrobes with the assistance of some of the wealthy women in the community

who donated more suitable attire for them to perform in. Though they continued to wear their

traditional post-slavery burlap and cotton attire, their new daywear was more casual than their

evening wear and often consisted of draped overskirts to produce an apron-like effect from the

front. When they performed in the evenings, however, the girls were adorned in European-

influenced, formal evening attire; all donated by the wealthy White women in their community

back home. The new, formal fashions featured pleats held by tape and supported by bustles, a type of framework used to expand the fullness or support of a drapery. Elaborate drapery in the back, tight fitting sleeves and square neck-lines completed the look. Their underskirts were heavily trimmed with pleats, flounces, rouching and frills. Their skirts were supported by a hybrid of the bustle and crinoline, a stiffened or structured petticoat or hooped petticoat, sometimes called a "crinolette".

They now wore low necklines and very short, off-the-shoulder sleeves, and they also adorned short or mid-length gloves. Unable to afford jewelry, they adorned their necks with velvet ribbon tied high around the neck and trailing, similar to today's choker necklaces.

The men wore shorter versions of frock coats which had become fashionable by then. These jackets were generally cut straight across the front and had collars and lapels. Under these coat jackets they sported vests which had also become popular by then. Staying in fashion, they wore dark, rather than white waistcoats, white bowties and a shirt with new winged collars. Full-length trousers were worn for most occasions. In 1873, Levi Strauss and Jacob Davis began manufacturing and selling original copper-riveted blue jeans in San Francisco, and the Professor managed to get each of the male singers one pair for casual attire.

They all had spent time imagining what it would be like abroad, and were excited to experience their first voyage at sea. They fantasized about the wonderful accommodations and gourmet meals they would be provided with on-board.

The Professor and Mrs. White cheerfully greeted the children as they arrived with their proud families, as did the Pastor and his wife. Mrs. White wore her finest pearls, a mink stole and a knitted hat covered her head. She had gloved hands and a White hankie.

Pastor Bennett led a prayer as the group held hands.

Dear Gracious, Heavenly Father. We come today just to say, 'thank you'. The students have worked long and hard, and are now about to experience one of the most exciting things that will probably ever happen to them. Give them stamina, Lord. Give them clarity, give them the ability to remember who they are and whose they are. Please keep their voices strong and their health good as they travel about your wonderful seas. Keep their families and parents safe while they are gone. Give those with dominion over them the ability to hear their concerns and to keep them safe. We trust you for safe travel, and we board the ship knowing that you are with us. We love you and give you all of the glory and honor you so rightfully deserve. In the name of the most holy one on high, amen and amen.

The children chattered excitedly as they boarded. They were anxious to see their cabins and looked forward to taking long, lazy walks on the ship's decks. Once aboard, they were met by a Purser.

"Welcome aboard the Holland America. We are happy to have you as our guests. Professor and Mrs. White, if you and the Bennetts would please follow my colleague, and the rest of you, please follow me this way." He turned and walked away, and they all followed.

"The Pastor and I are here as chaperones to the students, so we will be accompanying them to their quarters," Mrs. Bennett explained.

The Purser was confused, but he obliged. "As you wish, ma'am."

The group obediently followed the Purser down a long hallway adorned with impressive artwork and statues. They all looked on in amazement as they passed the dining room and smelled the aromas of prime meats and delicacies. They feasted their eyes on fancy desserts and huge, copper coffee urns. Fine china and silver utensils adorned the white linen-covered tables. When they reached the end of the long hall, the Purser led them down flight after flight of stairs.

"Where are they taking us?" someone asked.

"Where do you think?" Maggie snapped. "You didn't think they were going to let us lodge with the White folks, did you? They're taking us to the bowels of the ship to hide us away like stow-aways. I knew it. So much for the luxury trip we dreamed of. We will be traveling exactly like our enslaved forefathers; just aboard finer accommodations. White folks are White folks, and that will never change."

"Oh, Maggie. Don't be so critical. At least we're on-board. And we're going to Britain, for Heaven's sake. Can't you be satisfied with that?" Georgia retorted.

Some of the other students nodded in agreement with Georgia, and Maggie turned her nose up at them.

"No. I can't. You all can be satisfied if you want to be. But, I'm insulted. This is no different than sleeping in train stations and sneaking through back doors of sleazy hotels. I'm not satisfied at all."

Just as Maggie had predicted, when they reached the bottom of the stairs, they were in the steam room. The Purser led them around a corner, then ushered them to two small quarters; one for the males and one for the females. They entered the small quarters without complaint and found cots lined in a row.

"At least there is a cot for each of us," Maggie sighed.

They placed their bags underneath their cots and waited for further direction from the Pastor's wife.

"Settle in, children while I find out what time dinner will be served. You all might want to find something appropriate for the dining room."

With that said, she left the cabin to locate the Purser, who was dutifully standing by the door with his gloved hands folded in front of him.

"I've instructed the children to change their attire into something more appropriate for dinner. What time should I have them ready for dinner?"

"Oh. I beg your pardon, ma'am. The Coloreds won't be dining with our other guests. We will provide rations for them down here." He pointed to a corner near the steam room. "We set up some milk crates and shipping boxes they can use as tables and chairs, over here. I'll bring leftovers from the tables after each dining hour. Is there anything else I can assist you with?"

The Pastor's wife was speechless as she turned and stormed off.

"Very well. I'll be on my way. If you should need anything in my absence, please make note of it, and I will address your concerns when I return," he called out after her as she slammed the door to the lowly quarters he had accommodated them with.

#

Dear Mama,

You should see this huge ship! Even though our sleeping quarters are as small as a closet, the ship is the size of a building! I don't understand how it stays on top of the water, but thank God, it does. We have been sailing for many days, but I hear that we should be there soon. I miss you already.

Ella

The singers gave their first European concert in London where the Seventh Earl of Shaftesbury, a famous social reformer in Britain, agreed to sponsor the concert on behalf of the Freedmen's Missions Aid Society.

"I hope we are doing the right thing here," Ella Sheppard worried before one of their performances.

"What do you mean, Ella?" Minnie asked her.

"What if they don't like us, or our singing? What if they can't understand us, or the music?"

"As long as we do our best at what we do, they should enjoy our expert harmony and our classical presentation. Don't worry, Ella. We'll be just fine."

The concert went so well, in addition to singing for Queen Victoria and Prime Minister William Gladstone, they were also asked to sing for royal guests all over Europe. Queen Victoria wrote in her diary: *they are real Negros. They come from America and they were all once slaves. They sing extremely well together.*

Mrs. White hadn't been seen much since they boarded the ship, and the students missed her presence. However, out of respect, they did not question Professor White about her whereabouts. The students and the Professor kept up their rigorous rehearsal and performance schedules throughout the year, with the students returning in the evenings to their sub-standard accommodations.

After Mrs. Bennett got them settled, she and Pastor Bennett would usually meet Professor White and his wife in the dining hall for a luxurious dinner. This particular evening, Mrs. White arrived looking tired and weary, disheveled and detached. Her hat was merely sitting on top of a pile of un-styled hair, her shoes were not appropriate for the evening gown she was wearing, and the Professor was literally holding her up as they approached the table.

"Is she drunk?" Mrs. Bennett whispered to her husband as they approached.

"I most certainly hope not," he whispered back.

The Pastor stood and waited for Mrs. White to take her seat. She looked pale and weak, but she managed to force a smile.

"Sit, dear. I'll get you a cup of tea," the Professor consoled her, then he went to seek out the Server.

"Mrs. White, is everything okay?" Mrs. Bennett asked with great concern.

Before she could respond, Mrs. White retrieved a hankie from her purse and went into a fit of coughs that lasted nearly a full minute. Without realizing it, Mrs. Bennett had turned up her nose and was covering her face with one of her hankies, as not to contract any germs from Mrs. White. Just then, Professor White returned with the cup of tea and the Waiter.

"Good evening. What can I bring you fine folks?" he asked, his pad and pen ready to write down their requests.

"I'll have a lovely glass of your best red wine and the prime rib dinner," Mrs. Bennett nodded and smiled.

"And you, ma'am?" the server asked Mrs. White.

Just the thought of ordering the food made her stomach turn and caused her to feel nauseous. She quickly grabbed the lemon from the saucer that the tea was sitting on and bit into it, causing the nauseous feeling to pass.

"I'm fine. I don't care for anything, thank you," she told the waiter.

"Dear, you must eat. You haven't put anything into your stomach for days. I'm so worried about you," the Professor pleaded.

"I just can't bring myself to eat anything, George. I've never felt this ill in my entire life."

"I'm so sorry to hear that you're not feeling well, Mrs. White," the Pastor's wife said. "Exactly when did you fall ill?"

"Not until I got on this God forsaken vessel. I was just fine before then. Lately, I've come down with a fever, I don't have an appetite, and I spend most of my time in the ladies' lounge; if you know what I mean." She used the back of her gloved hand to wipe the perspiration from her forehead.

"I think you should see the ship's Doctor first thing tomorrow, Mrs. White. I've heard that these ships, elegant as they may look, can harbor all types of nasty germs. Maybe you've caught something aboard the ship," the Pastor suggested.

"That sounds like an excellent idea, Pastor. I think I'll call first thing in the morning and see if I can make an appointment. I think it's best that I take my wife back to our cabin and call for room service. Please, excuse us," the Professor apologized. With that, George White assisted Mrs. White up from the table and back to their cabin.

The next morning, the Professor was able to get Mrs. White an appointment to see the doctor. Feeling too ill to get fully dressed, he simply wrapped a long, warm robe around her on top of her night clothes, and they set off in the direction of the medical facility. The Doctor took them into his examining room, checked her over thoroughly, then asked the two of them to wait in the waiting area while he looked over his notes.

When he returned, the Doctor looked very serious and troubled.

"Professor White, Mrs. White," he began as he took his seat and referred to his notes as he explained the situation to them. "Unfortunately, Mrs. White has come down with what looks like typhoid fever."

Professor White straightened up in his seat. Mrs. White remained calm and lethargic. "What is this...*typhoid fever*?" White leaned forward and demanded, then shot off a series of questions. "I've never heard of such a thing. Are you sure? Is it curable? How did she contract it? She was fine when we boarded the ship last year."

"I'm sorry, Sir, but your wife may have very well contracted the disease aboard the ship."

"What!

"Yes, Sir. It can be caused by unsanitary drinking water or food. We made several announcements during our voyage regarding a possible outbreak, and asked that everyone come in to get checked out. We had those who were exhibiting signs of illness disembark at one of our previous ports."

Professor White suddenly remembered the grueling schedule they had been keeping over the year, and the many hours they were not within earshot of the public announcement system.

When they were onboard, they were usually rehearsing in the bowels of the ship, because the students were only allowed above deck if they were on their way to a performance. When they were performing, they were not aboard the ship, at all.

"Unfortunately, Sir, your wife has waited too long to come for treatment."

"Whatever do you mean?"

"I'm afraid there is nothing I can do to save her. She will eventually succumb to her condition."

The Professor brought both hands to his face, covered his eyes and began to sob uncontrollably. Mrs. White sat limply in her seat, not grasping the full nature of the situation.

"There must be something you can do! Is there no cure for this? There must be something you can do!"

"No. Unfortunately, as I have said, you've waited too late to bring her in. I can provide you with a small amount of ether to help with any pain, but that is all I can do. I'm so sorry, Professor."

The Professor collected Mrs. White out of the seat and assisted her back to their cabin. After he made her as comfortable as possible, he sent for Pastor Bennett who arrived and knocked softly on their cabin door.

"Come in," the Professor instructed him.

"Mr. White. How are you this fine day? And Mrs. White? My wife and I have been so worried about her health. Were you able to get her to the Physician today?"

"Yes, Sir, I was."

George White offered the Pastor a seat and poured two cups of tea. The two men sat in adjacent chairs, then White continued.

"I'm afraid I have some terrible news," the Professor announced, then broke into tears. The Pastor sat his tea cup down and went to console him, but White waved him away. "I'm fine. I'm fine, Sir."

"Please, tell me what's going on," the Pastor pleaded as he retook his seat.

"It's my wife, Sir. She has come down with something they call typhoid fever."

The Pastor rubbed his chin in contemplation. "I've read about this, George. People are cured from it all of the time. She'll be fine, I assure you."

"We waited too late, Sir. There's nothing they can do for her. The Doctor says she will eventually succumb to her condition. What have I done?"

Pastor Bennett rose from his chair. "Let us pray, Professor White. Prayer always helps in any situation."

"*Most Heavenly Father, our strength and our redeemer, my brother, George White needs you. We ask you, in the precious holy name of Jesus, to heal Mrs. White's body. Give her strength and a will to live and carry on. We trust you with all healing power and we beseech you to intercede on our behalf. Bless Professor White in his work here abroad, keep the students safe and well until we can return to our loved ones in America. Amen, and amen.*"

Thereafter, the Pastor would mention Mrs. White every morning during their morning prayer. Though they missed her presence, the students persevered and continued the work they had been sent to do.

One particular evening after their performance, they retired to their assigned meeting place to await the Professor's arrival with their agenda for the next day. Frustrated, they all began to express their true feelings regarding their stay abroad.

"I declare. Mr. Loudin may have been right, as much as I hate to admit it," Ella sighed as she plopped down on a chair and began to untie her shoe laces. "I am completely exhausted! We've been here for a year already. Surely they must be tired of us, by now. I'm ready to go home."

"I agree, Ella," Rutling, who usually just rolled with the punches and never complained, agreed. He loosened his bow tie and unbuttoned his vest. "I don't know how much longer I can go on like this. Sometimes I feel as though I could just…" Rutling stopped mid sentence and his body began to wobble. His knees buckled and he fell to the floor with a loud thud. The other students gasped as they jumped to their feet and went over to where he lay lifeless on the floor. Pastor Bennett directed someone to fetch Professor White, then he came to Thomas' aid.

"Oh Lord, Thomas is dead!" Maggie shouted. "He's dead, I say. These White folks have killed him. Which one of us is next?"

"Thomas. Thomas, are you okay?" Ella asked as she gently patted him on his cheek. "Please, say something."

"He's fine," Loudin announced as he pushed through the crowd. "He's fine. Give the man room to breathe."

Thomas began to stir and his eyes slowly opened and rolled around in his head. His speech was groggy as he managed to get the words out. "What's happening? One moment I was standing there. The next, I don't know what happened. I'm just so exhausted. Please don't fuss over me. I just need some rest."

"These White folks are killing us! That's what's happening," Maggie firmly stated.

Professor White entered the room as Thomas was being assisted up from the floor and placed in a chair.

"That's exactly what you need; some rest. That is what we all need," the Professor emphatically announced. "Since there are eleven of you now, maybe we can rotate singers each evening so that some of you can get some rest. Ella, I would appreciate it if you'd send an urgent telegram to the university asking for permission and funds to return home as soon as possible. Now, I must return to my wife's side. She' been very ill."

"Can I help, Professor? What would some of her symptoms be?" Rutling inquired.

"She's constantly complaining of headaches, she's weak and fatigued most of the time and she just can't seem to shake that nasty cough."

"I'm sorry, Sir, but that sounds like it may be Typhoid Fever. It's a very prevalent condition abroad. You might want to have her tended to by a Physician when we return to the states."

"If we ever get to return to the states," Minnie Tate attempted to complain. However, she had found it more and more difficult to speak, let alone sing, in the past few days. She had tried hot tea with lemon, hot water with lemon, then simply tried hot water alone. Nothing was helping, and every day her voice became weaker and weaker. This had caused her to sit out during several of the performances in the past few weeks as Mrs. Bennett attempted to nurse her back to health.

Benjamin Holmes had also developed a nagging cough in the recent weeks that kept him from performing, as Pastor Bennett attempted to nurse him back to health. His cough became so alarmingly unbearable that the Professor and the Pastor put some of their own money together and had Benjamin seen by the ship's doctor. It turned out that he had developed tuberculosis.

"You just take care of yourself, Thomas. I'll see to my wife. Now, let's all get some rest. We have a full day tomorrow," the Professor instructed them.

After the Professor left the room and the students began to file out, Maggie began to rant.

"They are killing us, you fools! That's what's going on. Killing us so they don' have to pay us. That's exactly what's going on," Maggie warned them, to no avail.

#

Dear Mama,

It is terrible here. So many bad things are happening, I wish I could just come home. The Professor's wife is ill, Thomas Rutling fainted, Frederick Loudin is still getting on my nerves and trying to buddy up to the Professor so that he can get my job, and Maggie Porter is still complaining. She thinks the school administrators are trying to kill us so they will not have to pay us. I never heard anything so ridiculous in my life! Why is it that some people can never be satisfied, mama?

Ella

CHAPTER SEVENTEEN

A bereaved Ella Sheppard showed up at Professor White's quarters carrying a tray that held a pot

of hot tea, honey and lemon slices. She sat the tray on the table next to the door, then knocked

lightly. She faintly heard Professor White tell her to come in, so she opened the door, picked up

the tray and proceeded into the room which was dimly lit and smelled of eucalyptus oil. Mr.

White was sitting in a chair by the bed, wrapped in a blanket. He suddenly began to cough

fiercely, as he held a white handkerchief over his nose and mouth. Ella sat the tray down on the

night table beside the bed, poured a cup of tea from the steaming pot and offered it to him. As

the Professor began to sip from the cup, Ella sat in a chair opposite him.

"I am so sorry about your wife, Professor White," she consoled, shaking her head. "She was very ill in her last days. Have peace knowing she was able to spend time in this beautiful place. You can rest assured she's resting with the Lord, now. Surely, you can find some peace in that."

"Thank you, Miss Sheppard. Your words do, indeed bring me comfort," he assured her as he sat the cup on the table and went into another fit of coughing.

"I declare, Sir. It is imperative that you make it to a Doctor soon," Ella pleaded as she offered him a fresh hankie from the night table.

As White disposed of the blood-stained hankie he had just used, he replied, "I've heard enough from Doctors. I just need to rest. By the way, have we heard from the university regarding our returning to the states?"

Ella stood and retrieved a letter from her pocket. "Yes Sir. We received a telegram from them earlier today. I have it right here," she said as she opened it and read:

'Your honorable Professor White, please accept our condolences in regards to the death of your lovely wife. The university has received your telegram requesting permission to return to the states with your most outstanding group. Please know that your efforts are greatly appreciated here, and we wish you continued success while abroad. On that note, we are proud and pleased to inform you that you have been granted permission to return to the states for a short time, at the end of your assignment, but have been invited back to Britain in the Spring. The university has gladly accepted the invitation, and we look forward to your safe travels home. Respectfully, Dean Cravath, in accordance with the A.M.A.'

George White jumped to his feet and the blanket fell to the floor. "Why, those most ungrateful, greedy…"

Before he could finish his sentence, he began to violently cough and held his hands to his chest as he sat back down. Once he regained his composure, he continued his rant.

"Have they no respect or sympathy for our talents? I can't go on like this, Ella. I just can't. You students are younger than I am. You must uphold our reputation and our commitment to the university. I must impose on you and ask that you take over during the remainder of our stay here. I must get better."

"Absolutely, Professor White," Ella assured him. "I'll take care of everything. You just rest and get better. I'll make sure we are prepared to complete our task. Now, you rest. I'll take care of everything," she said, and poured him another cup of tea.

"Thank you, Miss Sheppard. Thank you. Good night."

As she left his quarters, Ella cringed as she heard the Professor go into another fit of coughing. She shook her head and continued on her way.

When she reached her living quarters, Ella pulled Maggie to the side.

"Maggie, I need your help."

"I can't imagine what for, Ella."

"Professor White has taken ill, and he has put me in charge of the group."

Maggie gave her a dazed look.

"That means you have to step up and accompany us on the piano," Ella clarified.

"I will do no such thing!" "Why, I am an accomplished Soprano, Ella. Not a piano player."

Desperate not to have to deal with pompous Frederick Loudin, Ella tried a different approach. "Maggie, don't you see? If I take over Professor White's position, that moves you up to my position as Assistant Director. I know you don't want Frederick Loudin to step in, because you know he will. The next thing we know, he'll be in charge."

Maggie contemplated the situation momentarily, smiled and agreed. "I guess you're right, Ella. He's not a student at Fisk, anyway. Why should we give that old man the pleasure of bossing us around? Okay. I'll do it."

"Okay," Ella whispered. "Come with me while I tell the other students."

"I'm right behind you," Maggie assured her as they went to gather up the others.

Once everyone had assembled around, Ella stepped away from the crowd and faced them. Maggie stood dutifully by her side.

"I'm sorry to report that Professor White has taken ill," Ella announced.

Gasps and moans came from the crowd.

"Will he be okay?" someone asked.

"He is trying his best to get better. However, in his absence, he has left me in charge."

Some of the students applauded, some voiced their congratulations and some approached to pat Ella on the back.

"What? You are just a child! You couldn't possibly believe that you can handle this group," Loudin contested. "Surely, the Professor is delirious and not thinking clearly. I will speak to him at once! I'm sure he meant to place me over the group, Miss Sheppard."

"As you wish, Mr. Loudin. In the meantime, I am in charge. And, thus, Maggie Porter has become Assistant Director. If that doesn't suit you, you are more than welcome to return to the states. At your own expense, of course."

"Atta girl, Ella," Maggie encouraged her. "Don't you let him boss you around."

#

Dear Mama,

We are all sad here. Professor White's wife has died, and now Professor White has taken ill! He has put me in charge, and Frederick Loudin is having a problem with that. We still have another year to be here, then we've been granted permission to return home to the states for a short time. What, next? Oh, mama. I didn't know life could be so hard. I miss you very much.

Ella

#

After his wife's death, Professor White was grief-stricken. However, once he recuperated, he and the students continued on their quest to raise funds to save the university. They kept their rigorous schedule and performed night after night to appreciative crowds around Britain until one evening, after a performance, White collapsed. Thomas Rutling came to his rescue and tended to him until a real Doctor showed up.

"Step aside, young man. Step aside," the Doctor ordered. "What happened here?"

"The Professor has been under great emotional stress since his wife died last year, Sir, and we keep a very rigorous schedule. I notice lately that he has had a terrible cough, and one day I actually noticed his handkerchief was blood-stained after he covered his mouth during one of his coughing fits."

"Very good observations, young man. Are you a Doctor?"

"No, Sir. But I did have opportunity to work as a Surgeon's Assistant."

"You must have been an excellent student. This sounds like hemorrhaging in the lungs, but I won't know, for sure, until we run some tests. Please have him come to the medical facility first thing in the morning."

"I'll be sure to have him there, Sir," Loudin assured the Doctor.

The group continued on for another year in Britain under the direction of Ella Sheppard, keeping their promise to the university to send funds home to save their school. Thomas Rutling had several more unexplainable fainting spells, but had not yet determined what was causing them. At the end of their second year, and as they prepared to return to the states, Professor White received a communication from the Dean of Westminster. The letter read:

Dear Professor White,

As Dean of Westminster, it has come to my attention that your group will be returning to the states soon. Please know that we have enjoyed their performances tremendously, and are sorry to see you and the group depart. Your singers are both, talented and entertaining.

However, one singer in particular, who I have learned is named Isaac Dickerson, has enamored my interest. Therefore, on behalf of the University of Edinburgh, I have been given the authority of offering Mr. Dickerson an opportunity to stay in Britain to continue his studies, where his education will be fully funded.

Please notify Mr. Dickerson of our decision, and we await his reply.

Respectfully

CHAPTER EIGHTEEN

The students had persevered in Britain for two years. By the time they returned home, Minnie

Tate's voice had torn to shreds, Benjamin Holmes' nagging cough had been diagnosed as

tuberculosis, and once the Professor spoke with Isaac Dickerson regarding the most impressive

offer from the University of Edinburgh, Dickerson accepted their offer, quit the troupe and

pursued his studies.

After a few days of rest, they all returned to class and were glad to see one another. Once

again, they gave individual reports to the other students who hadn't gone on the trip. They

chattered about the size and elegance of the ship, their sub-standard accommodations, Rutling's

many fainting spells, the death of Professor White's wife, and the Professor's illness.

The students who had remained in the states chattered about the progress of the construction of the first brick and mortar building on the campus. Some speculated that it would be the administrative offices, others thought it might become housing for the students. They all agreed that the funds earned while abroad were being used to construct the building, which brought them great pride. Frederick Loudin entered the classroom and looked around.

"Miss Sheppard. How are you this fine day?" he asked.

Ella was busy preparing the music folders with sheet music. She moved from music stand to music stand in the process. Maggie Porter merely followed her, observing, but not helping.

"I've been better. Need some rest, but I just can't let Professor White down. He's depending on me to get us prepared for this next tour. I trust you're packed and ready to go? You do realize we depart for Europe in just two short weeks?" She stopped what she was doing and briefly met eyes with Loudin.

"Of course, I do, Miss Sheppard. And I trust you and the other members are also ready to embark on what might be the very tour that saves the university."

"About as ready as we'll ever get."

"Very well." Loudin turned his attention to Maggie Porter, who was now standing alone near her music stand, ruffling through her sheet music.

"Don't be in my business. Just take care of yourself," she snapped before Loudin got a word out.

"I'm sure it is an extra burden on you, with the Professor traveling while ill," he said, as he returned his attention to Ella. "I'd be more than happy to assist you in any way I can, Miss Sheppard. Just say the word."

"I'm sure you would, you sly dog," Maggie uttered under her breath.

"I'll be just fine, Mr. Loudin. Just fine," Ella assured him. "You just tend to yourself. I'll be just fine. Maggie, can you help me with the sheet music, please?"

"Ella, you are starting to worry me. What do you need me to get? You're always needing me to get something."

"I appreciate you Maggie. I really do."

"Lord, next you'll be asking me to carry your bags. Before I'm done, White folks will be carrying **my** bags."

Dean Cravath entered the room and looked around over the frame of his glasses.

"Well, well. I trust you students will have everything prepared to depart for your three-year European tour?"

"I believe the women-folk are seeing to that, Sir," Loudin assured him. Then he mumbled something under his breath that Dean Cravath couldn't quite make out.

"Excuse me, Mr. Loudin. Did I miss something you said?" Cravath asked.

As Maggie and Ella looked on in expectation, daring Loudin to speak his piece, he reached deep down inside and mustered up the courage to go toe-to-toe with Cravath.

"Since you asked, Sir, I must say, the pace the university is pushing us is inhumane. Professor White's health is a sure sign of that. As it is, both Benjamin Holmes and Minnie Tate's health has deteriorated, and both have been forced to quit the troupe. The university must respect our right to rest, and allow more time for us to remain in the states."

"Surprisingly, Mr. Loudin, I tend to agree with you on that point. Therefore, when the group returns to England, I will be taking over for Professor White."

A dead silence fell over the room.

"Very well. I will leave you all to your arrangements. Please let me know if I can be of any assistance," Cravath instructed as he turned and left the room.

Maggie and Ella looked at one another in shock. They were both speechless. Frederick Loudin, on the other hand, went into a rage.

"What! He's taking over the choir? First a woman, now the Dean of the university? Why, this is ludicrous! I will surely be informing Professor White of this travesty at once!"

#

That Spring of 1875, with just a few of the original singers and several new members, Professor White had regained his health and was able to accompany the students on a second tour of Europe. However, Dean Cravath also traveled with them. Because the students had made such an impression on their first visit, their arrival was anxiously anticipated by the British, drawing crowds in the 10,000's.

The following year, Professor White took the group to Holland. He didn't expect as successful of results as they had in Britain, because English was not a popular language there. He was pleasantly surprised, however, as the singers were mobbed by admirers all over Holland.

Once again, Professor White's health began to decline. In addition, Ella Sheppard became ill and wasn't able to stand in for the Professor. Dean Cravath stepped up and began to coordinate the choir. He placed Frederick Loudin in charge of directing and put Maggie Porter on the piano. He went to visit Professor White to assure him that everything was under control.

"Professor White, I'm sorry to hear about your health. However, you and the students have done a tremendous job raising funds for the university. What might I do to help?"

"Yes, the students have done an outstanding job for the university, Mr. Cravath. Last I heard, we are close to being out of debt." White paced back and forth, his arms folded behind his back as he spoke. "Therefore, I must appeal to you on behalf of the students, once again, Sir." He suddenly stopped and faced Dean Cravath. "The students must rest. They have literally been touring for *years* without rest." He pointed an accusatory finger toward the Dean, who politely listened to White's commentary. "I haven't forgotten that the school donated a mere $1 toward the student's efforts in the beginning. You must listen to me on this account. They will be no good to you if you continue at this pace," White warned.

"Nonsense. Utter nonsense," Cravath scoffed. "Why, they are professionals. We need them on the road. I will hear nothing of it." Cravath raised his arms in victory. "We've been invited all over Germany!"

"Well, you can count Ella Sheppard out. She's taken ill and is practically bed-ridden by a respiratory infection that's threatening to kill her."

"I've already placed Frederick Loudin into her position as your Assistant, and will find another soprano to replace her."

That said, Dean Cravath turned to leave. As if it had suddenly occurred to him, he spun around and faced the Professor.

"By the way, were you informed? Due to the institution falling into debt over the winter, the funding for the troupe has been cut off. Good day."

#

Dear Mama,

   What a beautiful country this is. We couldn't believe how many people came out to hear us sing, and they enjoyed us very much. Professor White was feeling better, and had begun to direct us again. But he took ill again, and Dean Cravath is now in charge. We finally made it to Holland and saw the wind mills there. We have a lot of new singers, now, so we have to rehearse extra hours so they have time to learn all of the music. I think we are making a lot of money, but I really wouldn't know if that's true. The Professor handles all of our financial matters. I hope everyone back in the states is doing well. I miss you all very much.

   Ella

#

Along with Dean Cravath, the students continued the tour all over Germany. This leg of the tour proved to be one of the most grueling of their trips, as it encompassed ninety-eight days, forty-one towns, and sixty-eight concerts. The students rehearsed all day and sang all night. When they returned to their living quarters, they never had a moment's peace. One singer had a stroke, Rutling continued to collapse, and petty arguments and spats broke out between several of the students; especially involving Maggie Porter.

Professor White had decided to call the students together one morning before rehearsal, as he had gotten wind that there was a lot of dissension among the singers, and he wanted to get things under control. Before he turned the corner and entered the area outside of their sleeping quarters, he could hear the mass chaos going on.

Maggie Porter and Frederick Loudin were involved in a heated debate in one corner. Pastor Bennett was attempting to intervene in their situation. Minnie Tate was bent over in a corner, vomiting and holding her stomach. Mrs. Bennett was attempting to tend to her needs. Ella Sheppard was so ill, she was confined to the bed, so she listened to the fiasco from underneath the covers. Thomas Rutling had fainted again and was spread out on the floor. Georgia Gordon was standing over him, screaming for someone to fetch Professor White.

"What is going on here?" White demanded when he reached the scene of near chaos.

"Thomas has fainted again. He needs help!" Georgia cried out.

By this time, Professor White had begun to carry a small vial of smelling salts in his pocket for situations just as this.

"For Heaven's sake," he muttered as he removed the vial and briefly waved it across Thomas' nose.

Thomas began to stir, then he slowly regained consciousness and was assisted off of the floor. White then turned his attention to Frederick Loudin and Maggie Porter, who were still going toe-to-toe in the corner. Pastor Bennett had given up on their situation and was now assisting Rutling to a chair. Maggie reached back and took a stance to slap Mr. Loudin in the face.

"Miss Porter!" Professor White yelled as he interceded and caught her arm. She spun around, surprised.

"Miss, Maggie Porter," she corrected the Professor as Loudin took the opportunity to walk away.

"Whatever are you two arguing about, now?" White demanded.

Maggie collected herself and straightened out her dress. "Mr. Loudin seems to think that he is your Assistant, now that Ella Sheppard is down. I was merely trying to relay to him that Ella's duties revert to me, not to him," she scowled at Loudin as she spoke.

"Surely, that is no reason to result to violence, Miss Porter. You were about to strike the man in the face, for Heaven's sake!"

"That's because he said something vulgar and vile to me," she pointed a finger in Loudin's direction.

"I dare ask, what did he say?" the Professor cautiously questioned, rubbing his brow.

"He said that one of these days, my mouth was going to get my posterior in trouble. How dare he speak to me in that manner!"

Though the Professor agreed with Mr. Loudin's assessment, he was not about to insult Maggie, again. She was already more upset than he had ever seen her. However, with no intentions of speaking with Mr. Loudin regarding this situation, he patronized Maggie, in order to keep the peace.

"I will speak to him, at once, Miss Porter, and explain to him that his behavior was out of line."

"*And* that I will be assisting you, now that Ella Sheppard is ill," Maggie demanded.

"Precisely. Now, can we all pull it together and get to our rehearsal hall?" the Professor pleaded with the entire group.

Though he tried, the students became resistant to Professor White's attempt to keep order. In May 1878, Professor White had had enough. He and Frederick Loudin clandestinely met at a bistro while ashore, outside of the earshot of the Bennetts and Dean Cravath. Over a cup of fine, roasted coffee, the two men were able to momentarily exhale the pent up frustration they were experiencing during this leg of the tour. The students were tired, ill, and physically and emotionally run down.

"Thank you for meeting with me, Mr. Loudin," Professor White sighed as he prepared his coffee with cream and sugar. He slowly began to turn the silver spoon in a circular motion as he stared into the cup. Loudin had begun to take his coffee black, so he merely picked up his cup and took a sip.

"Certainly, Sir. I, too, so needed a break from all of the chaos. This was an excellent idea."

The two men enjoyed their coffees as they listened to a man softly playing a piano in the corner of the room. They briefly enveloped themselves in the music.

"Oh, to be able to merely sit here for an evening and enjoy someone else's performance for a change," White chuckled.

"It is glorious, Sir. However, we need to address the concerns of the group and decide how we will go on with so many singers ill and defiant." Loudin sipped his coffee, then sat back in his chair before he continued. "I can't say that I much blame them, though, Sir. The university has been most unfair in not compensating us outside of our tuition fees for our tireless efforts."

"I wholeheartedly agree with you, Mr. Loudin," the Professor admitted. "Outside of the $40 we received from the A.M.A., the $1 we received from the university and the $30 or so dollars I pitched in to launch our first tour, the university has financially abandoned us over the years."

The two men shook their heads in shame, then returned their attention to the piano player as his musical piece crescendoed to a close. They politely clapped, along with the other guests, then continued their conversation.

"How would you like to handle this, Sir? You have my full support. Just tell me what I can do to help," Loudin offered.

By this time, the two men had forged a very strong relationship, and Frederick Loudin supported Professor White, wholeheartedly, in his position regarding the troupe's right to rest and renumeration. Professor White privately leaned on Loudin for emotional and professional support, as not to offend Maggie Porter and Ella Sheppard.

The musician started to play another classical tune as the men continued their conversation. The Server arrived and freshened their cups of coffee.

"I think it best that I confront Dean Cravath head-on, and voice my position on behalf of the students. I've had it with him and the university's unfair treatment, and if I can't get them to listen to reason, I'm prepared to end my relationship with the university."

Loudin was not expecting to hear this from the Professor, as he had no idea that White felt this strongly regarding the maltreatment the students were receiving from the school administrators. He leaned forward in his chair and intently looked White in the eyes. "Are you sure that is what you want to do, Sir? You've done such a miraculous job with the group, I would hate to see you make a decision you might regret later."

"Believe me, Frederick. I have spent many countless nights rueing over some of the decisions I've made in the past regarding the group and my wife, for that matter."

Loudin sat back in his seat.

"I understand, Sir. It has been a trying decade, indeed. Please know that I support your position, wholeheartedly, and I'm prepared to support you by terminating my relationship with the university, also, if that is the decision you ultimately come to."

Professor White's face showed alarm. "I won't let you do that, Mr. Loudin. You have a wonderful career under way, and the group so needs your talent to be complete. I will not hear of it. This is my mess and my fight.'

"But, whatever will you do, Professor?"

"Oh, I've made plenty of contacts over the years. I can return to any of several churches in Ohio or remain in Nashville and teach at another institution. The groundwork has been done, and many universities now offer Liberal Arts to newly-freed students."

As the pianist ended, yet another beautiful rendition, the patrons courteously applauded, then Professor White and Loudin rose from their seats. Professor White left $1 bill on the table, the two men tipped their hats to the Server, then placed them on their heads and stepped out onto the street. As they strolled along, they finalized their conversation.

"I would be more than happy to approach Dean Cravath with you, Sir, as a representative of the other students," Loudin suggested.

"That might be a good idea, Mr. Loudin. I'll let you know before I approach Mr. Cravath. Now, let's get back to the ship. I'm sure the others are wondering where we have ventured off to, by now."

"Certainly, Sir. This has been a refreshing outing. Thank you for the invite."

"My pleasure, Frederick."

With that, the two men returned to the ship, having made a pact to approach Dean Cravath together in a joint effort to get him to listen to reason. After they boarded, they happened to run into the Dean coming down the hallway. Loudin gave White a raised eyebrow and White returned the gesture. As the Dean approached, the two men ambushed him.

"Mr. Cravath, we must speak to you at once!"

"Mr. White. So good to see you up and around."

He merely looked at Frederick Loudin and acknowledged his presence.

"And you, Sir. I must speak to you about the singers."

"Why, of course, Professor White. Shall we go to my cabin?"

"No, thank you Sir. I'll be brief. I've come to speak to you about a raise in pay for the singers. They have worked very hard for the university, and though the tour has been a huge success, several members have become ill, they are being asked to keep up a rigorous schedule, and none of the students have been compensated relative to their talents and contributions."

Cravath listened intently, but did not respond. He allowed Professor White to finalize his thoughts.

George White counted with his fingers as he made point after point of his argument to the Dean. Loudin merely stood by in moral support.

"Thomas Rutling collapsed again last night, and all are exhausted. I'm doing my utterly best to keep order, but several of the members have become resistant. By my calculations, we've contributed at least $50,000 to the university this year, alone! Now, surely you and the board should be able to see your way to an increase and a time of rest."

"Precisely," Frederick Loudin chimed.

Cravath folded his arms across his chest and paused briefly before answering.

"Professor White, I'm sure you have the best interest of the singers at heart, but the funds just aren't there right now."

"If that, indeed, is the case, I'm afraid I must render my intention to terminate my relationship with the choir and the university."

"As I, Sir," Loudin added.

"As sorry as I would be to see that happen, Professor White, suit yourself. There will be no increases in pay or suspension of the remaining tour. Good day to both of you."

"Very well, Sir. Then I will be on my way."

"As I," Loudin added to no avail.

"As you see fit, gentlemen."

The two men left Dean Cravath standing in the hallway and stormed down the hall.

"We don't need them, Sir," Frederick Loudin scoffed as they went their way. "We can re-organize the group on our own. As you said earlier, we have made all of the contacts we need to carry on without the university's support, *or non-support,* for that matter. You are not the only one that has kept a log of contacts over the years, Sir. I must admit that I have quite a respectable collection of contacts, myself."

"You may be right, Mr. Loudin."

"I know I'm right, Sir. With the assistance of my lovely wife to keep our itinerary and the books, we can strike out on our own."

"But, what will we call ourselves?" the Professor inquired.

"Why, of course we will call ourselves the Fisk Jubilee Singers. We need the name recognition."

"Very well," White agreed. "You speak with the other students and feel them out regarding their moving on with us, and we will carry on. Thank you for your support over the years, Mr. Loudin. Your input has been priceless. Until we meet again. I will be returning to the states forthwith."

"As you see fit, Sir. I will stay behind and attempt to keep the group together and the tour on track. I don't hold out much hope, however, as President Cravath, Ella Sheppard and I seem to butt heads on every turn. And then there is that phenomenon called Maggie Porter to contend with."

"Do your best, Frederick. Just do your best."

"Good night, Sir," Loudin said as the men shook hands, then turned to leave. Frederick Loudin departed filling victorious. He would finally get the opportunity to show what he could do with the choir.

The next morning, Loudin couldn't wait to announce to the students that he was now in charge of the group. After they had their morning prayer and scriptures, he went up to the front of the room.

"Good morning, everyone."

Loudin barely got the words out before all havoc broke loose.

"Where's Professor White?" someone asked.

"Professor White will no longer be in charge of the troupe."

"What!"

"Whatever will we do?

"What happened?"

"Who is in charge, now?"

"Is he okay?

"Is he dead?"

The questions came so rapidly, Loudin couldn't tell who was asking what.

"He has quit the group and the university. Ella Sheppard has taken ill, and the Professor and I have have agreed to form our own troupe and continue touring, once we return to the states."

Idle chatter broke out among the students as they looked at one another in shock.

"Then, I quit, too!" Maggie shouted.

Oh, for that to be true, Loudin thought. That would most certainly make his life easier, and the other students would be easier to manage. On the other hand, he thought it best not to comment, and moved on.

"As each of you have already proven your talents, you are all welcome to be part of the new troupe, once it is organized. I will need definite answers from you, however, before we return to the states. There is much work to be done."

"I'm not singing under that woman-demeaner," Maggie whispered to Thomas Rutling.

"I don't know, Maggie. I'm actually thinking of remaining here in Germany. It's such a beautiful and interesting place. I'd like to explore more of it, if I could. What better time than now?"

"Really?" Maggie surprisingly asked "What a novel idea, Thomas. Whatever will you do here, though? Do you plan to perform?"

"I'm going to keep my options open, for now. I'd like to rest my voice and put myself under a Doctor's care to find out why I keep fainting, and I have a brochure of a wonderful walking tour that sounds divine. I just might venture out on it. Why don't you stay here with me, Maggie? Think of all the fun we could have, traveling on our own with no one to tell us when to come or when to go."

"I don't know, Thomas. With Loudin taking over, that might be a good idea. I'll give it some thought and let you know."

"That would be great."

#

When Professor White disembarked the ship to return to the states, Pastor Bennett and his wife did likewise. Two months later, after she returned to the states, Ella Sheppard also left the group for six weeks after she almost died from her respiratory infection. Maggie Porter took Thomas Rutling up on his offer and remained in Germany, and Isaac Dickerson had remained in Britain. Albeit, the original Fisk Jubilee Singers had disbanded.

Their final tour as the original Fisk Jubilee Singers raised a total of $150,000 for the university. These funds were used to finish the construction of the first permanent structure for the education of African-Americans, and was given the name, "Jubilee Hall", in honor of the students who had toiled tirelessly for the university. The building is now designated a national

historical landmark, and a floor-to-ceiling portrait of the original Fisk Jubilee Singers hangs in

it's lobby. The portrait was commissioned by Queen Victoria during their tour of 1873 as a gift

to thank them for coming.

CHAPTER NINETEEN

When Professor White, along with Frederick Loudin, formed the new group of Jubilee Singers they had previously discussed while abroad, they heard that Maggie Porter had returned to the states, and Professor White asked her to join up with their group, totally contrary to Frederick Loudin's wishes. Now Assistant Director of the group, Loudin attempted to reign the singers in to create a more polished presentation. His being in charge did not sit well with Maggie Porter, however. As if it were Loudin's fault, she complained about every aspect of his authority and the continued unfair treatment they experienced. She complained about the tireless hours of rehearsals, the rate of pay, the quality of meals, transportation and lodging. Her biggest complaint, however, was concerning the overt racism they still were experiencing on the road.

Additional members included Jennie Jackson, Mabel Lewis, Patti Malone, Hinton Alexander, Benjamin W. Thomas and newcomers like R.A. Jall, Mattie Lawrence and George E. Barrett. The newly-formed group was making appearances in Tennessee, and one particular afternoon they boarded the train to take a short ride from Nashville to Memphis. As they had taken this trip many times, they knew where the *Coloreds Only* seats were, and went to their respective riding car. However, as there were not enough *Colored Only* seats available in the female car, Maggie Porter sat in one of the last two seats in the car marked *Whites Only,* next to a White girl who was already sitting there. The girl stood, turned her nose up at Maggie and the other girls, then left the car.

"More room for me," Maggie smarted and crossed her legs, pulled a book from her satchel and began to read.

A large, black cloud of smoke rose from the engine of the train, then the train bucked, the wheels slowly started to turn and they slowly crept out of the station. Some of the girls began to have polite conversation, others delved into books they had brought along.

They had ridden along for a while, then stopped at a station to take on more passengers. Before long, a young, White girl entered the car and looked around for a place to sit. She noticed Maggie sitting in one of the seats marked 'Whites only'. The girl walked up to Maggie, who was still engrossed in her reading, and said, "Excuse me, but you need to move, nigger."

Maggie turned her attention away from the book and looked the girl up and down.

"I beg your pardon?" she asked, appalled.

"Oh, my God," Minnie told Georgia. "This is not going to be good. This is not going to be good, at all," she predicted.

"It most certainly isn't," Georgia agreed as they looked on.

"I said," the girl snapped. "You need to move, nigger. These seats are for Whites only. Can't you read?"

Maggie slowly closed her book and put it in her satchel. Then she stood to her feet and walked up so close to the girl, she nearly stepped on her toes.

"Don't you dare call me a nigger. My name is Maggie. Miss, Maggie Porter, White girl. I have traveled this world, twice, singing for Queens, dignitaries and politicians. I have put up with racism, prejudice and mistreatment from you White folks all of my life, and I am not putting up with it any longer." Maggie stomped her foot and the other girls startled. "Now, if there were not another seat there, and you had asked me nicely, I might have kindly given you this seat. After all, it is clearly marked 'for Whites only'. Yes, I can read. However, since you have been so rude to insult me and call me a nigger, you can go find yourself a seat somewhere else."

With that said, Maggie used her gloved hands to straighten her hat, adjusted her shawl and returned to her seat. She retrieved her book out of her satchel, opened it, looked at the girl briefly, then continued to read. At a loss for words, the White girl stomped her foot, turned and stormed out of the car.

The other girls from the group were left with their mouths gaping after witnessing Maggie's bold exchange with the girl.

"Maggie, we need to get out of here. There's going to be trouble, indeed, if that White girl comes back," Georgia warned.

"You cowards can run, if you like, but I'm not going anywhere. This is the free south and I'm done running and dealing with disrespect."

The train was still sitting in the station when the door to their car opened and the conductor was on the other side of it. The White girl was close on his heels, rapidly chattering off her version of the incident. The conductor gestured for the White girl to calm herself, then turned his attention to Maggie.

"Are you the Colored girl who offended Miss Laurie, gal?"

Maggie boldly looked at the conductor. "Yes, I am the Colored girl who put little Miss Laurie in her place, and my name is Miss, Maggie Porter, not *gal*."

"Then, I'm afraid you gals are going to have to leave the train."

The other girls stood and left the car immediately. Maggie, however, stood her ground.

"We have paid our fares and are holding valid tickets. This is not our station, and we are not leaving the train."

"See, what did I tell you? She's a smart-ass little nigger girl. I want her off of the train," the girl whined.

"Gal, we don't want any trouble. I need you to disembark the train, at once, or I will have to call for assistance."

Maggie stood and planted herself firmly in front of the conductor.

"I told you, my name is not *gal*. It's Miss, Maggie Porter."

Just then, the other girls returned with Frederick Loudin, and the male singers.

"Excuse me, Sir. What seems to be the problem?" Loudin asked the conductor.

The conductor turned and faced him.

"Is this gal traveling with you?"

"Yes, she is. We are the world renowned Fisk Jubilee Singers, on our way to a performance in Memphis."

"I don't care who you are. This gal is sitting in a 'Whites only' seat, and she insulted Miss Laurie. I have kindly asked her to disembark the train, and she is refusing."

Loudin reached into his pocket and retrieved a $1 bill before proceeding. He discreetly folded the bill, then offered it to the conductor.

"I'm sure we can straighten this out, Sir. Please give me a minute to speak with Miss Porter. "

The conductor accepted the bill, slipped it into his pocket, then sneered at Maggie. "There is no straightening out needed. I want this gal and her friends removed from the train."

With that, the conductor put a whistle up to his mouth and blew into it. Before long, several White, male employees showed up at the car. They abruptly pushed Loudin and the male singers to the side, then grabbed each of the girls by the arm, including Maggie Porter.

"Get your filthy hands off of me, you heathens. How dare you! Remove your hands from my person!" Maggie protested.

Amid much protest from Loudin and the other male singers, the girls and Miss, Maggie Porter were man-handled, ushered through the aisle for all to see, then literally pushed off the train, whereas they fell to the ground in their beautiful performance dresses, as the steps had been taken up. The girls began to cry as they picked themselves and their hats and purses up, and brushed off their dresses. They adjusted their hats and wiped their tears with their dirt-soiled gloves as they watched the train jerk and slowly pull out of the station, leaving them stranded and alone.

"Now, look what you've done, Maggie," Georgia complained.

"Look at our dresses," Minnie whined.

"Oh, stop your whining, you babies. They are not going to get away with this. I'm going to make them pay. One day, they will wish they had never heard the name, Miss, Maggie Porter."

"I already wish that day were here," Georgia snapped.

#

In addition to not getting along with the other singers, Maggie Porter often forgot her lines, showed up late for rehearsals, and when she did arrive, she always upset the flow of the rehearsals with her 'diva' antics. One day when Maggie showed up late and unprepared, Frederick Loudin called her to the side after rehearsal.

"Miss Porter. May I speak with you, please?"

"Seems as though you are already speaking to me, Mr. Loudin. What do you want?"

"I'd like to speak with you regarding your attitude and behavior."

"There's nothing wrong with my attitude *or* my behavior. What ever are you talking about?"

"Miss Porter," Loudin hesitated. "Ever since the day I met you, you have always seemed to resent being a member of this ensemble, and defiant to the authority placed over you."

"Make your point, Mr. Loudin."

"I'm afraid that the troupe can no longer put up with your unwillingness to get along with the other singers. And your outright defiance and attitude toward our accommodations and our rigorous rehearsal and performance schedules is totally unprofessional and unacceptable. Not to mention the recent episode on the train."

"I have carried this group for over eleven years as a stellar soprano, a piano accompanist, and Assistant Director, Mr. Loudin. It was only my commitment to the university that kept me involved with this troupe, instead of striking out on my own as a solo performer. If you will recall, I remained in Germany after our last tour with Dean Cravath, and I only returned to the states because Professor White wrote me and asked that I return to join the newly-formed group that the two of you put together."

Loudin is at a loss for words. Maggie is not. She continued.

"I don't need you to chastise me regarding any aspects of my behavior. We have tolerated ridicule, racism, and downright disrespect our entire careers, and I passed on a very lucrative career of my own to remain a member of this group. If you are looking for an apology, I'm sorry, but I don't have one for you. Is there anything else I can help you with, Mr. Loudin?"

Loudin paused momentarily and collected his temper and his thoughts before responding to Maggie's commentary. "I'm sorry that you feel that way, Maggie. However, now that Professor White and I have joined forces and formed the new group, I assure you that things are going to be changing for the better. Our contacts and professional relationships have paved the way for us to demand better accommodations, better pay and overall better treatment. Compounded with my wife's most efficient record-keeping and our Agent's capable booking experience, I can assure you that things will be different from here on out."

"You can believe that, if you like, Mr. Loudin. However, I am of the belief that White folks are White folks, and that is simply a fact that you need to accept. I have put up with all of the mistreatment I plan to put up with, and from here on out, I will demand equal rights and equal pay for my services."

"Unfortunately, Miss Porter, if that is still your position, I must suspend you from the group for six months. We cannot move forward with singers who harbor that type of negative attitude. We will contact you after your suspension, if we require your further assistance."

Maggie could not believe what she was hearing. She stared Frederick Loudin down for a full moment. "Very well, Mr. Loudin," she smarted. "But, the group will not be successful without me. You mark my word."

Maggie threw her fox-tailed boa over her shoulder, adjusted her hat, then turned and stormed off.

CHAPTER TWENTY

A group of influential Black men planned to convene, with no affiliation with either the Democrats or Republicans, but as free independent American citizens, for the purpose of presenting to the country the grievances of the Colored people. They had made plans to discuss weather newly-freed Coloreds in the South should be assisted in migrating to the north, as racism was still running rampant in the South. Kansas was welcoming the Southerners with open arms. At the time, Coloreds in the South; namely the state of Texas, were still being treated unjustly in business, employment and housing. There were no voting rights, wages were slave-wages, and housing was not made affordable. As a result, hundreds of thousands of ex-slaves were fleeing Texas and moving North, thus causing financial strain on the Southern farmers' ability to sow and reap their crops.

The Whites, and some Blacks, were blaming the Republicans for inciting the Southerners into leaving Texas in droves by encouraging them to relocate to other areas where racism was not as prevalent. Things were escalating to the point that the country was, likely, facing financial ruin, and maybe even another civil war. Frederick Loudin hadn't forgotten about the maltreatment the women of the Jubilee Singers had suffered on the train earlier that year. As a result, when he got wind of this upcoming conference of Black men, scheduled to be held in Nashville, he made note of the dates and location of the event, and made plans to attend as a Delegate from Pittsburgh. Loudin surmised that this would be the perfect forum to present the Jubilee Singers' plight regarding the issues they had with the railroad system, and he hoped to get the subject on the agenda.

The delegate met at the state capitol in Nashville, Tennessee on May 6, 7, 8 and 9, 1879. Great care was taken to not mischaracterize the gathering as a *convention*. The meeting was formally referred to as "The National Conference of Colored Men of the United States", and was believed to be one of the most interesting and important assemblies ever convened in America at that time.

After the attendance was taken and officers were elected, the conference started with much testosterone-filled dialogue as the gentlemen jockeyed for position on the speaking platform. Some females also attended the conference, and at one point, a gentleman stated that there were a number of ladies standing, while gentlemen were sitting. Several men stood to allow the women to sit, and they moved on.

Ever the businessman, Frederick Loudin had arranged for the Jubilee Singers to be present. As a result, as part of the opening-day session, a gentleman briefly eulogized the

Jubilee singers, then resolved that they be requested to perform one or two songs. This was adopted unanimously, and the Jubilee Singers entered the hall and were introduced to the Conference amid great applause. Under Frederick Loudin's direction, they sang "Steal Away to Jesus", which was rendered in splendid style, followed by a burst of applause.

Steal away, steal away, steal away to Jesus.

Steal away, steal away home,

I ain't got long to stay here.

My Lord, He calls me,

He calls me by the thunder,

The trumpet sounds within-a my soul.

I ain't got long to stay here.

Green trees are bending,

Po' sinner stand a-trembling,

The trumpet sounds within-a my soul,

I ain't got long to stay here.

They followed up with "In Bright Mansions", which included their infamous recitation of The "Lord's Prayer". The acoustics of the building made their voices sound angelic, and they were applauded for a full three minutes as they gave their bows.

Many topics were discussed and many resolutions were made over the four days of this history-making conference, whose minutes was taken daily and published in the local *American* newspaper. The next day, the newspaper's account would be resolved and accepted as an accurate account of what happened during the conference the previous day. Those minutes were ultimately submitted, and are currently maintained at the Library of Congress.

During one session, statistics quoting the revenue from the sale of cotton, sugar, molasses, rice and tobacco were read. In 1878, these revenues totaled $177,298,930; of the manual and other labor, expenditures for the same totaled a mere $158,000. Over hours and hours of speeches, debates, insults, apologies, discussions and resolutions that spanned over the four days, much was resolved. It was resolved that Colored people should migrate to those states and territories where they could enjoy all the rights which were guaranteed by the laws and constitution of the United States, and enforced by the Executive departments of such states and territories. It was resolved that we (the Black race) ask of Congress of the United States an appropriation of $500,000 to aid in the removal of our people from the south. It was resolved that June 19th be set aside as a Colored national holiday and celebrated as the anniversary date of emancipation. It was resolved that we ask publications to use a capital "N" when typing the word Negro.

When it was finally resolved and accepted 'that the action of the railroad conductors, in forcibly ejecting the ladies of the Jubilee Singers from the ladies' car, merits our undivided condemnation', Frederick Loudin and the Jubilee Singers stood and took their bows as the crowd applauded.

A gentleman from Illinois offered: *"whereas we have listened with sorrow and regret to the remarks of the gentleman from Tennessee, recounting the cruel and uncivil manner in which the Jubilee Singers have been recently treated by employees of one of the railroad companies of this State; therefore resolved that we, the representatives of the Colored people denounce and condemn such acts as being indecent and inhuman in the extreme, and that the persons*

committing the same deserve the censure and condemnation of all good citizens, irrespective of

sex, color or nationality."

When it came time to adopt the resolution, a voice was heard from the audience saying, "I object!"

Gasps were heard all around the hall. Many of the gentlemen, and all of the women in attendance stood to their feet and began to look in all directions to try to pinpoint where the objection came from. A gentleman from Tennessee couldn't believe that someone objected, and boldly blurted out.

"Who said that?"

A gentleman from Texas arose and looked in all directions. He asked, over and over again, "Who objected to that? I want him to stand up; I would like to see him."

There was a good deal of excitement, then the man stood up and confessed. It was the gentleman from Georgia.

"I am the man, and as good a man as ever wore a pair of number sixes. I 'm sorry, but I thought that I was objecting to something else to which I was opposed. I withdraw my objection."

Once that issue was cleared, the resolutions continued, and it was resolved that legal counsel would be secured to sue the railroad in Federal court regarding the female Jubilee Singers. To bring the suit would cost $500. Frederick Loudin of Pittsburgh was appointed to this committee.

A gentleman from Kentucky changed the subject and stated that "slavery is not *dead*, it is just *sleeping* in the south" and "that we pay no heed to such men as Fred Douglas and his accomplices, for the simple reason that they are well-to-do Northern men who will not travel out of their way to benefit the suffering Southern Negro, and who care not for the interest of their race." At the end of the fourth day, much had been said, much had been accomplished, however, much had been left unresolved.

#

Businessman that he was, Frederick Loudin had hired A. Cushing as an Agent to take charge of the new group's bookings. He had also put his wife in charge of the financial matters for the group. This group, too, was successful, as Loudin led them on a two-year tour to Asia, Australia and the America West during the 1880s.

In 1881, the newly-formed Jubilee Singers performed In Chattaqua, New York, some 30 miles away from Manhattan. On this particular evening, Professor White took the stage, directed the students through a stellar performance, turned to the audience to take his bow, and fell from the stage. Frederick Loudin, who was standing nearest to White, immediately dismounted the stage and went to his rescue. The audience gasped and looked on in despair. Pastor Bennett and his wife, who had rejoined the group when they returned to the states, immediately went on bent knees and began to pray. All of the students left the stage and came to White's rescue. When they arrived by his side, the Professor was unconscious.

"Step aside, step aside. Give him room," Loudin demanded, then turned his attention to the audience and asked, "Is there a Doctor in the house?"

A stately gentleman broke through the crowd and came to the Professor's aide to assess his injuries. The crowd of students moved away to let the Doctor through as they all looked on with worry and concern.

"This was bound to happen," one of the female students whispered to Maggie, who had just rejoined the group after her six month suspension.

"I must say, I agree with you. He's been so ill lately. I don't know why he just won't let it go. Performing nearly every night is bound to take it's toll on all of us," Maggie predicted.

"Well, at least we are being compensated for our time. Unlike touring for the university," the other student reasoned.

"George, George," Loudin called out in a panic. He dropped down by White's side and grabbed him by the shoulders. "Wake up, Professor. Please, wake up," he pleaded with sincere concern.

The Doctor pulled a small vial from his pocket, opened it and briefly waved it under Professor White's nose. White stirred, grunted, then slowly opened his eyes. The Doctor checked Professor White's vitals and looked for any broken bones. "I think his ankle is sprained, but not broken."

"George, can you stand?" Loudin asked.

George White sat up with the assistance of the Doctor and Loudin, then they assisted him to his feet.

"I'm fine. I am fine, Frederick. Thank all of you for your assistance. Let's get back to our lodging. I will be just fine."

Loudin and one of the other male singers took White by each arm, assisted him backstage and helped him sit.

"What happened, Professor?" Maggie asked.

"I don't know, Maggie. I became dizzy, then lost my footing. I'm fine, now. I'm fine."

"Are you able to continue, Sir? I'm willing to step in and lead us the remainder of the way," Maggie suggested.

"I see the tables have turned now, Miss Porter," Loudin ridiculed. "Your services won't be needed. This troupe belongs to Professor White and myself. Therefore, I will be taking over for the Professor."

"Therefore, Mr. Loudin, Miss, Maggie Porter will be taking her leave." Good bye," she said, then turned and walked away, never to sing with Loudin's group again.

CHAPTER TWENTY-ONE

Ella Sheppard returned from her six-week leave in 1878 after recuperating from her illness. Once she learned that Fredrick Loudin was now in charge, she quit the group, altogether and married George Moore, who was also a Fisk graduate, that same year. The Moores lived in Oberlin, Ohio while George studied for a degree in Divinity. They started a family and became the parents of a son they named Clinton Fisk Moore, after the school's founder, Clinton B. Fisk.

In 1883, Ella and George moved to Washington, D.C. to a neighborhood they were very proud to be members of. Ella was reminded of the fond memories of their stay at the Wormley Hotel, and the two settled into their new home and took time out to explore their neighborhood, often taking leisure strolls in the early evening air. One evening as they walked along, hand-in-hand, they passed the doorway of one of the business establishments as a drunken man came falling out and landed at Ella's feet, prompting George to valiantly grab Ella by the elbow and remove her from harm's way in the nick of time as the drunken patron fell to the ground with a thud.

"My God," she exclaimed. "Is he sick, or drunk?"

"Probably a bit of both, dear. Come along," George instructed her as they crossed the street and continued.

Ella looked back over her shoulder, once they were safely on the other side, and read the sign on the building which read, "The Good Time Saloon."

"No wonder," she told George. "It's a watering hole. And here's another one!" she exclaimed as they passed the entryway of another business and caught the scent of hard liquor and tobacco reeking from the building as someone opened the door to exit.

"And another one just ahead on the other side of the street," George added.

By the time they reached home, the Moores had counted five such establishments within the few blocks they had walked. Upon further investigation, they learned that there were at least thirteen such establishments in close proximity of their home.

By this time, George had become ordained as a Pastor and was currently teaching Theology at Howard University. He and Ella felt compelled to take up the cause to transform the neighborhood into a more acceptable area to raise a family, and led a temperance campaign against the thirteen saloons. They also became advocates for the social advancement of African Americans, and their efforts were successful and helped transform the neighborhood into one of D.C.'s most prominent areas today.

In 1892, Ella and George Moore moved back to Nashville and built a home across from Fisk's campus. They both renewed their relationship with the university where Ella assisted various choirs and sometimes sang, herself. Ella became a researcher and lecturer on African-American and women's issues, and she also lent her voice and her pen to such organizations as the American Missionary Association (A.M.A.) and the National Association of Colored Women.

In addition to her various social and political activities, Ella paid for the education of several Fisk students, including her half sister. She continued to take care of her mother and raised both her youngest son and a niece that had moved in with the couple when she was four.

The Moores became friends with several well-known African-American intellectual couples such as Frederick and Helen Douglass and Booker T. and Margaret Murray Washington. As did Frederick Loudin.

#

In 1884, as George White never fully recovered after his fall, Frederick Loudin formed a new group of singers and launched a six-year world tour. He called his group the Loudin Jubilee Singers, and he was very selective about his singers at this time. He even had his wife conduct investigations into their backgrounds before he allowed them to join the troupe. Under Loudin's leadership, and with his wife aboard, the group was now entirely composed of, and run by African-Americans. Loudin led this choir to England, Ireland, Australia, New Zealand, India, Singapore, China, Japan, and finally the American West.

Because of his wife's excellent management skills, this tour was so successful that Loudin and his singers were able to retire comfortably when the tour was over.

In 1893 Loudin, once again, served as a delegate to the National Conference of Black men. That same year, he joined anti-lynching journalist Ida B. Wells-Barnett who was

Born in Holly Springs, Mississippi July 16, 1862, a daughter of slaves, Ida B. Wells who was a journalist, newspaper editor, sociologist, suffragist, feminist, Georgist and an early leader in the Civil Rights Movement. In the1890s, she led an anti-lynching crusade in the United States. In other words, Ida B. Wells-Barnett was 'every' woman.

Loudin also joined forces with Frederick Douglass, an orator, social reformer, statesman and abolitionist whose intelligence served to disprove the notion that slaves were inferior and could not be educated. Without his approval, Douglas became the first African-American to be nominated to run for Vice-President of the United States on the *Equal Rights Party* ticket. One of his most famous quotes was: "*I would unite with anybody to do right and with nobody to do wrong.*" White people found it hard to believe that an ex-slave could speak and write so eloquently.

Loudin eventually returned to his hometown of Ravenna, Ohio where he became the owner of two shoe manufacturing companies. On November 2, 1892, the F.J. Loudin Boot and Shoe Manufacturing Company was dedicated in Ravenna. By April 1893 the company employed an integrated staff of nearly 70 men. This was a revolutionary act in Ravenna in the 1890s. These workers were able to make 150 pairs of shoes per day. In the end, however, the company was not able to stay solvent and was bankrupt within one year of opening which caused Loudin to ultimately close up shop.

Fortunately, during this time, the Loudin Jubilee Singers were still on the road touring and earning money for him, making it possible for Loudin to build his family a home in Ravenna. Though he was involved in many ventures, Loudin continued to tour with his troupe, every now and then, for the next twelve years.

CHAPTER TWENTY-TWO

After sitting next to Daniel that wonderful evening on their Baltimore stop of their 1871 tour, Maggie Porter and Daniel Cole were discretely inseparable and eventually married and had two sons and an invalid daughter. After their sons graduated from high school, as a French citizen, her eldest son joined the French army. Their youngest son, however, enrolled into the University of Michigan and began his studies. With only their invalid daughter remaining in the household, the Coles found themselves with more time on their hands than they cared to have. Over breakfast and morning coffee, Maggie struck up a conversation with Daniel.

"Dear, I'm bored and longing for something to fill my time."

Daniel continued to read his paper as he answered, "That's good, dear."

"Daniel!

Daniel lowered the newspaper and gave Maggie his attention.

"I'm trying to speak to you about a very important decision I'm considering. Please, pay attention."

Daniel set the paper down on the table and gave his wife his attention. "What have you decided, dear?

"I've decided to get the troupe back together."

"What troupe do you mean? The Jubilee Singers?"

"Yes. I've been thinking, why don't we start our own chapter of Jubilee Singers?"

"Do you really think that's a good idea, Maggie. It involves a lot of work, a lot of money, a lot of rehearsals, and time away from home. Furthermore, where would we ever get a group of singers capable of performing to our level?"

"It requires no more or less work than the work we put into being part of the Fisk Jubilee Singers."

"But, you need contacts, dear. We don't have any contacts in that world anymore."

Maggie arose from the table and briefly left the room. When she returned, she was holding a small black book which she waved in front of Daniel's face as she took her seat.

"Speak for yourself. Maybe you don't have any contacts, but I have plenty of them."

"There's so much to be considered, Maggie. How will we get bookings? Who will accompany us on piano? Who will direct? How will we travel? You know how much you hate segregated transportation. And don't even mention lodging. Where will we stay?"

"Oh, Daniel. Don't be so negative. I'll work out all of the details later. Right now, I just need to know that I have your support."

Daniel rubbed his brow and gave the idea some serious thought. He did miss the road, troubling though it had been at times. He missed the cheering crowds and the fuss they made over them as their performances began to be celebrated around the world.

"You work out all of the details, dear, and I will give it some serious thought."

"So, are you saying I have your support?" Maggie crossed her fingers in hopes that he would say yes.

"Of course, dear. If that would make you happy, you have my support."

"Thank you, Daniel. I'll get to work contacting some of the singers from the original Fisk Jubilee Singers, and find out if they'd be interested in joining us."

"Very well, dear."

Daniel returned to his newspaper and Maggie left the room to begin work. With a need for some well-trained singers, she penned letters to Georgia Gordon, Jennie Jackson and Minnie Tate, inviting them for tea.

When the women arrived at Maggie's home, they were not surprised to see that she had done quite well for herself, as her home was stately and grand. The colonial estate was set on massive, manicured grounds, and Maggie had Asian gardeners tending to her landscaping. The large, white columns leading up the many steps to the front door made the house look even grander. The entire front of the home was embellished with beautiful, white french doors with small window panes. A cedar wood porch wrapped around the entire house. There were various colors of rose bushes, uniformly grouped by color on one side of the property. On the other side were orchard trees bearing oranges, lemons, limes, peaches and even a cherry tree. In the distance and going up a hillside was a grape vineyard.

The three ladies looked at one another in awe as they took in the massive estate. When they finally arrived at the huge double doors, Georgia Gordon sheepishly pushed the button to ring the bell. Suddenly, they heard Beethoven chiming on the other side of the door and the three women looked at one another with raised eyebrows.

"Do you think she has maids, too?" Jennie Jackson whispered to them as they waited.

"I wouldn't doubt it, if she could find someone she could get along with," Minnie Tate whispered, and they all laughed.

The door slowly opened, and sure enough, a Black woman in a maid's uniform appeared.

"May I help you ladies?" she politely asked.

"Yes, we are here to see Maggie," Georgia answered.

The woman looked at them with confusion. "Maggie?" she asked.

"Yes," Minnie assured her. "Miss, Maggie Porter."

"Oh! Mrs. Cole. Come in, ladies. Please come in. Mrs. Cole is expecting you in the sun room."

The sun room? Minnie mouthed. *Mrs. Cole?* Georgia mouthed back, and they all quietly laughed. The Maid ushered the three women past a sitting room, then led them down a long hall that had walls adorned with old photos of the original Fisk Jubilee Singers. Maggie had gone to the trouble to have all of the photos hung in chronological order. The three women slowed their pace and took in all of the memories. It felt as though they were reliving their lives.

"Remember this one, Georgia? That's in New York at Beecher's church. We were just young girls then. My, has time flown by," Minnie reminisced.

"Yes, it has. But I wouldn't trade anything to have those days back again. They tried to work us to death, and almost did," Georgia teared up at the thought. "I remember this one," she fondly recalled.

"That's when we sang in the lobby at the Colored-owned hotel in Washington, D.C.!" Minnie shouted with glee.

"Yeah, after they kicked us out of the Georgetown," Georgia sarcastically reminded.

The Maid waited patiently as they perused every picture on the wall, seemingly having a story behind every photo. Their descriptions of events were so vivid, the Maid could see herself traveling with them. She merely stood by and dutifully waited. When they were done, she turned and continued to lead them to the sun room. They passed the kitchen where wonderful aromas made their way to their noses. They peeked in and noticed Maggie had a personal chef preparing her meal. They looked at one another again with raised eyebrows. When they finally reached the sun room, they saw Maggie giving instructions to a young lady dressed in a fancy business suit. Maggie looked up as they entered and were announced by the Maid.

"Excuse me, Mrs. Cole, your guests are here," she announced.

"Thank you, that will be all," Maggie briefly told the young lady she had been speaking to, who nodded at the three women on her way out, then left the room, closing the door behind her. Maggie then turned her attention to her guests.

The Maid stood at attention nearby, awaiting further instruction, or to be dismissed.

"Georgia, Minnie, Jennie! Oh, my God! It's so good to see you ladies again. My, have we all grown up!" Maggie approached them with opened arms and all three of the women greeted her with a hug.

"Maggie Porter," Georgia stated as she stood back and looked at Maggie.

"*Miss,* Maggie Porter," Minnie corrected her, and they all laughed.

"Actually," Maggie informed them as she showed them her ring, "it's Mrs. Maggie Cole, now. I married Daniel."

"Daniel Cole of the Jubilee Singers?" Minnie asked in a shocked tone.

"That's the one," Maggie bragged. You and Georgia weren't the only two holding hands with the fellas under the table back in Baltimore," she bragged. "Sit, ladies. Sit."

Maggie directed them to three comfortable chairs, then the Maid moved in and immediately poured each of them a tall glass of sweet tea. The ladies quietly sipped their tea as Maggie sat across from them and began to tell them why she had summoned them.

"Well, ladies. I'm sure you're wondering why I've called you here today, and you know I'm not good at beating around the bush, so I will not belabor the subject. Daniel and I are thinking about starting up another Jubilee Singers ensemble. We so miss performing and the wonderful travel experiences."

The ladies quietly sipped their tea as they listened intently. "Daniel has managed to put together a skeleton troupe from different choirs around town, but I think we need some established, professional singers," Maggie continued.

The ladies continued to quietly sip their tea, and Maggie sensed that they were not catching on to what she was trying to convey to them.

"Like you ladies," she finally divulged.

Georgia Gordon almost choked on her drink, Jennie Jackson shifted uncomfortably in her chair, and Minnie Tate's eyes grew as large as melons.

"Maggie, are you asking us to join up with you and Daniel?" Minnie shouted out.

Neither of the ladies readily answered as they thought about how neither of them had done much chorale singing since the group disbanded post Frederick Loudin's reign. Each of them had attempted to strike out on their own, but they had settled into retirement with the funds they earned during their tours with Loudin, so they hadn't given another thought to starting or joining another troupe.

"Well, say something, ladies."

"I don't know, Maggie. You know the two of us never really got along," Georgia admitted as she sat her tea cup on the marble table nearby.

"Oh, don't let that stop you, Georgia. I didn't get along with anyone. I still don't, if you rub me the wrong way," Maggie unapologetically admitted.

All three women laughed, took sips of their tea, then Maggie continued.

"That's because I wasn't willing to just idly sit by and endure the mistreatment the White folks constantly forced on us. The rest of you were complacent and long-suffering, and I don't judge you because of that. That just wasn't my style. Thank God for school. I would have made a terrible slave."

"But, where will we sing, what will we call ourselves, how will we get engagements?" doubtful Minnie shot off question after question, clearly interested in the proposition.

"I've thought about all of that," Maggie assured them. "The young lady who just left is my Agent and Personal Assistant. I've turned over all of the contacts I collected over those years, of nearly every venue we performed in, here and abroad. She will be contacting them on our behalf, in an attempt to book us a tour."

"You kept up with that stuff all these years, Maggie?" Jennie asked.

"Sure. How do you think I was able to find you ladies? Even though I couldn't stand the ground he walked on, I noticed that Frederick Loudin made a habit of saving the programs from every venue we performed at. He always kept a pen or pencil handy, and he would work the crowd and find someone to gain further contact information from, for future use. So, I took up the same practice behind the old fart's back."

"Maggie, you are before your time. But, you're also a very bold and smart lady. I would be honored to join your new troupe," Georgia announced.

"Well, if Georgia's in, so am I," Minnie laughed.

"You ladies are not going to leave me behind. I'm in, too," Jennie said and raised her glass of tea in preparation for a toast.

The four ladies clinked their glasses together, and it was official.

In 1884, when Maggie and Daniel finalized the roster of their singers, there were so many of them from the old group, they also called themselves the Fisk Jubilee Singers and toured the U.S., Canada and Europe between 1884 and the 1890's.

While traveling abroad, Daniel received a telegram one day which he hastily stuffed into his pocket before reading it. He and Maggie had many more pressing matters to attend to, and he planned to read the telegram later that evening, along with the other communications they received that day. Later, as they prepared to retire for the evening, Daniel remembered the telegram in his pocket and took it out and read it. Maggie entered the room as the paper he was holding fell to the floor. Daniel dropped to his knees and began to cry.

"No, no, no," he repeated. "God, please! no,"

Maggie ran to his side. "What is it, Daniel? What's happened?"

Daniel wasn't able to answer her, but he picked the telegram up from the floor and handed it to her. Maggie slowly opened it and tried to console Daniel at the same time, rubbing him on the back. She read the telegram:

Dear Mr. and Mrs Cole,

It is with our sincere regret and condolences that we inform you that your beloved son has perished while in battle for the French Government. Please contact the French Embassy as soon as possible to make arrangements to travel to France for his internment. Please let us know how we can accommodate you in your time of bereavement. Our prayers are with you.

Maggie let the paper fall to the floor, knelt down next to her husband and they cried together.

After the loss of their eldest son, the Coles traveled to France and endured burying their child. His death took a toll on their health, so they took time off of the road to grieve. From that point on, they kept in closer contact with their youngest son who was still attending the University of Michigan. Previously, they would receive communications from him from time to time, and as long as his tuition was paid, they rarely troubled him, assuming no news was good news.

One evening as they were watching television, the regular programming was interrupted as the words, 'news bulletin' flashed across the screen.

"What's going on, now?" Maggie sarcastically asked Daniel, who was an avid news reader and watcher. As he had been dozing, Daniel had the volume down low, so he rose and went to the television to turn the knob, thereby raising the volume so they could hear.

"There has been an incident on the campus of the University of Michigan. Preliminary reports from reliable sources are reporting that a young, male, Negro student has been found dead on the campus. We will bring you further details as they come in. Stay tuned."

Thinking back to the son they had already lost, worry immediately overcame them as Maggie and Daniel sprung to their feet and looked for the phone number to the university. They shuffled through several sheets of paper until they found some literature from the university. Daniel looked it over and over as the paper nervously shook in his hands.

"Let me have it, dear." Maggie said. "You're upset. Sit down. I'll find the number."

Maggie looked over the paper briefly, while Daniel took his seat and began to pray. She saw a phone number for the admissions office, carefully dialed the number and waited for someone to answer. She patted Daniel's hand while they waited. A woman's voice finally came over the receiver.

"University of Michigan Admission's Office. How may I help you?"

"Hello. This is Mrs. Maggie Cole. My husband and I just saw a news bulletin regarding an incident on the campus, and we would like to find out if our son is okay."

"What is your son's name, ma'am?"

Maggie didn't want to continue the conversation, as she got a sinking feeling in her soul and she didn't want to hear the answer. She held her breath and rubbed Daniel's hand harder as she answered.

"Daniel. His name is Daniel Cole."

There was a long silence on the other end.

"Hello?" Maggie checked to see if the woman was still on the line.

"Yes, ma'am," the woman hesitated. "You and Mr. Cole might want to make your way to the campus as soon as you can."

"Why?" Maggie snapped.

"That is all that I can say right now, Mrs. Cole. I'm sorry."

"Please get a message to our son to have him call his parents immediately," Maggie demanded.

"As I said, it's probably best if you and Mr. Cole make your way to the campus, ma'am."

Maggie dropped the phone receiver and Daniel picked it up and put it to his ear.

"This is Mr. Daniel Cole. Please, tell us what is going on."

"As I informed your wife, Sir, it is imperative that the two of you make your way to the campus. Please let us know when you have made travel arrangements, and we will have a car waiting to bring you to the campus. I'm sorry, Sir. My deepest condolences," she said, then disconnected the call.

CHAPTER TWENTY-THREE

In 1895, Professor George White died of tuberculosis. At his funeral service on Fisk's campus, several of the original Fisk Jubilee Singers were in attendance and sang "Steal away," a longtime favorite of the Professor's.

#

Isaac Dickerson died suddenly in 1900 of an aortic aneurism at the young age of forty-eight. At his service, the Stratford Grove Baptist choir sang songs that had been made popular by the Fisk Jubilee singers.

#

Frederick Loudin's successful career spanned nearly thirty years. In the Fall of 1902, Loudin collapsed while on tour in Scotland. He returned to Ravenna, where he died two years later, on November 3, 1904.

#

Thomas Rutling collapsed several times during their final tour of Germany, so once the original ensemble disbanded, he took a six-week walking tour of Switzerland, recovered his health and took up performing again. He taught himself French and decided to pursue the study of languages. He also spent time in Italy, then eventually returned to England where he attempted to give concerts for a living. Things did not work out, however, as no one abroad had really ever heard of Thomas Rutling. They only recognized the name of the Fisk Jubilee Singers. Rutling passed away in Harrowgate on April 26, 1915.

#

Ella Sheppard died that same year, 1915, in Nashville. By that time, she had reached her potential in intellect, in spirit, and in musical attainment, and was one of the truly gifted women of the world.

#

After the death of their second son, Maggie and Daniel Cole returned to the states and relocated to Detroit where they spent several months grieving his death. The Coles also moved their invalid daughter, who had been attempting to gain her independence by moving into her own flat, back into their home when she became less and less able to take care of herself. Thereafter, they settled into a retired life.

Though she lived in Detroit, some 500 plus miles from the Fisk University campus, Fisk sent Maggie a communication in 1931 asking her to return to Fisk to lend her time and talents to the university. By now, Maggie had learned much about negotiating and fighting for what she wanted. In her negotiations with the university, refusing to ride segregated trains and buses, Maggie demanded a driver pick her up in Detroit and drive her back to the university in Tennessee each time she visited.

Maggie Porter was revered by the students for her success as a singer, and she eventually became the last surviving member of the original Fisk Jubilee Singers. As an elderly woman she moved into a Phyllis Wheately home in Detroit where a niece of, none other than Frederick

Loudin was on the board, and took extra special care of her until she died in 1942.

Every year on October 6, they still celebrate Jubilee Day on Fisk's campus in these

students' honor. Not only did these pioneers open the world's eyes to a genre of music that is

still celebrated around the world, their persistence and the respect they gained as first class

entertainers played a role in de-segregating hotels, steam ships, railways and boards of education.

////

THE END

BIOGRAPHY

OF

JAMIMA BEATRICE JONES,

AUTHOR/PLAYWRIGHT

Born in 1955 in Los Angeles, and raised on the tumultuous streets of Compton, CA in the

mid 1960s, Author and Playwright, Jamima Beatrice Jones is no stranger to the literary dream.

After high school, she attended San Jose State University from 1973 to 1977, and while there

studying Business Administration Jones tried her hand at writing. This was right around the time

"Rocky" hit the screen, and Jones was intrigued that Sylvester Stallone both wrote and acted in the production. Feeling she could do as well as, if not a better job, in penning a story than Stallone, Jones wrote her first manuscript, "Bones". The title came from her college room-mate's nick name for Jones because of her, then, thin stature. Several rejection letters later she returned her focus to her studies.

Jones feels her most creative fictional piece was a short-story poem, "The Queen and Her Castle", a poetic tale of a Queen who, one day, received a visit from a strange Prince who wanted to explore her kingdom. The Queen took the Prince on a tour of her enchanted land, directing him to first look through her "windows", cross over her "mountains", and to stop at her "pearly gates" to rest. The Queen fell asleep while the Prince was exploring her gates, and the Prince touched her gates in a way that made them open and expose her "valley". The Prince pleasured himself in her valley and fled feeling victorious. However, when the Queen awakened she laughed and quipped, "after all, it was all just for fun".

Jones then wrote a fictional piece, "Project E3", right around the time of Pablo Escobar's reign and the coining of the term, "drug war". Project E3 told the story of two secret agents who penetrated Escobar's cocaine fields and contaminated the crop so that the drugs would render themselves useless on the streets. After a successful mission, the agents returned home just in time to be sent out on their next mission, because a new drug had just hit the scene. The new drug was called "ice". The $800 reading fee she invested resulted in, yet, another rejection letter.

Right around 2004 during her youngest son's junior year of high school, he came home one evening and said, in a nonchalant tone, "Oh, by the way, mom, I auditioned for and got into a group of Jubilee Singers". In as equal of a nonchalant tone, Jones replied, "That's great, son. What are the Jubilee Singers"?

"I don't know. I just know we sing a'capella and I get paid", was his response.

Jones eventually made it to one of his performances with this most elite and celebrated ensemble, and what she witnessed was a group of talented African-American singers dressed in semi-formal attire, singing spirituals with a classical twist. The director that evening gave a brief explanation of the source of the music, but didn't dwell on the significance of the group of newly-freed teens they were emulating. Years later, that same nonchalant son informed Jones that this same ensemble was looking to hire a Personnel Coordinator. Interested in applying for the the position, Jones prepared to interview by researching, via the internet, who the Fisk Jubilee Singers were. The deeper she dug, the more intrigued she became. With Wikipedia being the main source of her information into the backgrounds of Ella Sheppard, Maggie Porter, Thomas Rutling, Frederick Loudin and their Professor, George White and what they accomplished, her life was forever transformed as she uncovered the experiences of these brave, enduring youngsters and their untiring efforts to preserve the right to education for generations to come. Their efforts not only saved today's Fisk University from bankruptcy, but earned enough funds to construct the first-ever permanent structure for the education of African-Americans, Jubilee Hall, and introduced the world to spirituals. This research was ground zero for the penning of "The Story of Jubilee".

Originally written as a stage production, "The Story of Jubilee" debuted to a sold-out audience on October 6, 2010, seven years to the day that this biography is being penned. On the journey of it's creation, the most profound thing that occurred happened while Jones was searching for a photo of a river bank to be used as the backdrop for the scene of Ella Sheppard's near-drowning. Jones viewed several photos on the internet and settled on one she thought most likely looked like the actual river bank. Upon further research of the photo she selected, she learned that the riverbank is located outside of Queen Victoria's castle and had recently been named the "Jubilee River." Ironic, because Queen Victoria sent for the original Fisk Jubilee singers twice during their existence, and if you visit Jubilee Hall on Fisk's campus, there is a floor-to-ceiling mural of the original Fisk Jubilee Singers at the entrance, commissioned by Queen Victoria, to thank them for their visits.

In addition to her interest in writing, Jones is a licensed Realtor in the state of California since 2005, she has owned and operated a successful Tax Consulting firm since 1982, and during the 1984 Olympic games in Los Angeles and the 1996 Olympic games in Atlanta she successfully vended souvenir pins to thousands who came out to see the torch pass by. She also proudly served as Chief Merchandiser to the late, legendary Ray Charles during the last four years of his career. As Chief Merchandiser, Jones toured with Mr. Charles and met thousands and thousands of people. It is her belief that she has met someone from all fifty of the United States.

In 2012 Jones and her husband of 34 years relocated from Los Angeles to Palm Springs, CA where they currently reside. Because the move slowed down the efforts to continue the production as a stage play, her husband encouraged her to re-write the manuscript as a novel and submit it for publication, which is where we are today. It is her dire deSire to return this epic legacy to it's original purpose and tour the production as a perpetual stage play. Jones envisions Jennifer Hudson as Maggie Porter and Beyonce' as Ella Sheppard. A business plan has already been drawn up and the world awaits our arrival. All aboard. First stop, Cincinnati.

Made in the USA
San Bernardino, CA
20 March 2019